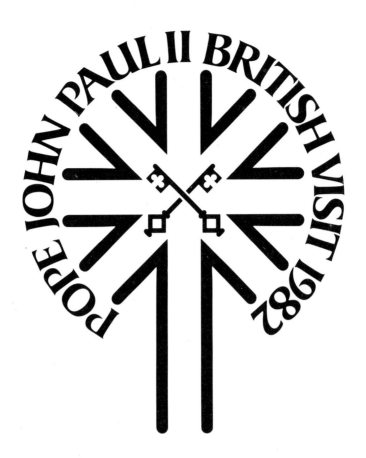

POPE JOHN PAUL II BRITISH VISIT 1982

THE POPE IN BRITAIN

PETER JENNINGS & EAMONN McCABE

FOREWORDS BY CARDINAL HUME & CARDINAL GRAY

THE BODLEY HEAD
LONDON SYDNEY
TORONTO

THE POPE IN BRITAIN

British Library Cataloguing
in Publication Data
Jennings, Peter
The Pope in Britain.
1. John Paul II, *Pope* 2. Popes —
Voyages and travels — Great Britain
I. Title
282'.092'4 BX1378.5
ISBN 0-370-30925-1
Nihil obstat Anton Cowan, Censor
Imprimatur Rt Rev. Philip Harvey, V.G., O.B.E.,
Bishop in North London, Westminster 13 June 1982
The *Nihil obstat* and *Imprimatur* are a declaration that a book or pamphlet is considered to
be free from doctrinal or moral error. It is not implied that those who have granted the *Nihil
obstat* and *Imprimatur* agree with the contents, opinions or statements expressed.
©Papal Visits Limited 1982
Text (excluding extracts and comments) ©Peter Jennings 1982
Photographs ©Eamonn McCabe 1982,
except photographs on pp. 27, 39, 41, 42, 44, 46, 49, 62, 69,
78, 83, 86, 96, 98 ©Arturo Mari 1982;
on pp. 10, 123 ©JS Library International
This book has been edited, designed and produced by
Aurum Press Limited
11 Garrick Street, London WC2E 9AR
Colour separations by Latent Image
Typeset by York House Typographic, Hanwell, London
and printed in Belgium
by Henri Proost & Cie PVBA for
The Bodley Head Limited
9 Bow Street, London WC2E 7AL
First published 1982

Acknowledgements

It is not possible to mention all the people who have helped me in the preparation of this book
but I should like to thank all those who have contributed, and the following for their generous
help, advice and encouragement:
Cardinal Basil Hume, Archbishop of Westminster; The Most Rev. Derek Worlock, Archbishop
of Liverpool; The Rt Rev. Alan Clark, Bishop of East Anglia; Mgr George Leonard, personal
assistant to Cardinal Hume; Mgr Ralph Brown, national co-ordinator, papal visit to England and
Wales; Most Rev. Bruno Heim, Pro-Nuncio to Great Britain, and his secretary Rev. Kieran
Conry; Rev. Patrick Olivier, Rev. Kevin O'Connell and members of the Catholic Information
Office of England and Wales; Rev. Alberic Stacpoole, O.S.B., of Ampleforth and St Benet's
Hall, Oxford; Cardinal Gordon Gray, Archbishop of St Andrews and Edinburgh; The Most
Rev. Thomas Winning, Archbishop of Glasgow; Rev. Daniel Hart, executive director, papal
visit to Scotland; Rev. Tom Connelly, director, Catholic press office, Scotland; Rev. Henry
Docherty, priest of the diocese of Motherwell; Dr Robert Runcie, Archbishop of Canterbury;
Canon Christopher Hill, ecumenical assistant to the Archbishop of Canterbury; Mr John Miles,
chief information officer, Church of England, and press secretary to the Archbishop of
Canterbury; Rev. Dr Philip Morgan, General Secretary, British Council of Churches. In Rome:
Bishop Agnellus Andrew, O.F.M., vice-president of the Pontifical Commission for Social
Communications; Rev. Romeo Panciroli, director, Vatican press office; Mgr Charles Burns,
Vatican secret archives; Rev. Lambert Greenan, O.P., Editor, English language edition of
L'Osservatore Romano; Archbishop Paul Marcinkus, head of the Vatican bank; Mgr John
Magee, Papal Master of Ceremonies; Mgr Richard Stewart, staff member, Secretariat for
Promoting Christian Unity.
  A special thank you to Aurum Press, and most of all to my wife Stella, a committed member of
the Church of England who drew great encouragement from the Pope's words in York: 'You live
in your marriage the hopes and difficulties of the path to Christian unity.'   Peter Jennings

***Previous page:* Pope John Paul II with Cardinal Basil Hume, Archbishop of
Westminster, and Cardinal Gordon Gray, Archbishop of St Andrews and
Edinburgh**

CONTENTS

FOREWORDS

Cardinal Basil Hume, Archbishop of Westminster
Cardinal Gordon Gray, Archbishop of St Andrews and Edinburgh

8

THE PAPACY OF JOHN PAUL II

11

CHRISTIAN UNITY

Interviews with church leaders

23

BACKGROUND TO THE VISIT

35

THE PASTORAL VISIT

The Pope's itinerary and extracts from
major speeches

40

REACTIONS

'Nothing will ever be the same again'

117

APPENDIX

Succession of Roman Pontiffs
Succession of Archbishops of Canterbury

127

My love
be with you all
in Christ Jesus
(I Cor 16, 23)

Joannes Paulus PP. II

Pastoral Visit to Great Britain

18 May – 2 June 1982.

The official Coat of Arms adopted by Pope John Paul II after his election in 1978, designed and executed by Archbishop Bruno B. Heim, the Holy See's Authority on all heraldic matters. His Excellency submitted nine different designs. The Holy Father chose to retain the letter 'M' (for Mary) which he had borne as Archbishop of Cracow instead of adopting the suggested heraldic devices for the Blessed Virgin from the Litany. Only Polish, and to some degree Swiss, heraldry allows ornate letters as an heraldic charge.

FOREWORDS

Cardinal Basil Hume, Archbishop of Westminster

The planning of the visit occupied almost two years. A small army — largely made up of volunteers — worked with an energy and attention to detail that was quite remarkable. There were many frustrations and uncertainties. The near-fatal assassination attempt on the Pope in May 1981 caused widespread shock and dismay; it left us for a long time doubtful whether the planned visit could ever take place. There was also opposition from groups of extremists. In fact, however, as the story unfolded, the major obstacle to the pastoral visit came from an unexpected quarter. It is now public knowledge that the conflict in the South Atlantic nearly caused the cancellation of the visit. Despite those who advised caution and postponement, Pope John Paul was impressed by the long spiritual preparation within the Catholic community, by the profoundly pastoral nature of the visit and by its ecumenical importance to relationships between the Churches in Britain.

The six days spent by Pope John Paul in Britain are sure to find a permanent place in the history and folk-memory of the people of England, Scotland and Wales. They would have been remembered — if for nothing else — by the mere fact that the pastoral visit of a Pope took place at all. But this visit merits far more than such formal recognition.

It was for the Roman Catholic community a celebration and confirmation of the Faith. The Holy Father prayed with his people, celebrated Mass with them, administered the sacraments to them and pointed the way forward on their pilgrimage. He came to help them renew their commitment to Christ and to his teaching. He brought them to the well-springs of the Christian life.

It was for other Christians much more than confirmation of the movement towards Christian unity. Pope John Paul caused profound satisfaction, delight and some astonishment by his ecumenical sensitivity, his sureness of touch, and the obvious rapport between himself and the British Christians who welcomed him so generously.

It was for the general public an unexpected festival of joy and the Spirit. People warmed to the Pope's goodness, his sincerity, his obvious concern and love for children and for all who suffer or are handicapped. Young and old seemed to find in him an affirmation of what is deepest and most valued in other human beings.

Finally, to believers and unbelievers alike, these days became a pilgrimage for peace. The conflict in the Falklands spurred the Pope to make repeated appeals for peace; he prayed for the victims of the war and their families; he rejected, especially in that striking sermon at Coventry, the idea that modern warfare can be acceptable as a means of settling international disputes.

It is too early to assess how the long-term effects of this quite remarkable visit will manifest themselves: sufficient for the present that we accept the whole experience with thanksgiving, humility and joy.

8

Cardinal Gordon Gray, Archbishop of St Andrews and Edinburgh

I am ploughing through a mountain of mail. Every letter is an expression of joyful thanks to His Holiness, Pope John Paul II, for all that he is and for all that he has done during his pastoral visit to Great Britain. There are letters from Catholics, but the majority have come from our non-Catholic friends: letters expressing admiration and affection for a man of God whose transparent sincerity, whose integrity and whose love for God and for each one of us shine forth like a beacon pointing the way to God; admiration for a man of peace, a herald of peace with the simple message of Jesus that we should love one another.

I write from my native Edinburgh, a lovely city of lovely people, but a city of people who are sometimes regarded as just a little undemonstrative, a people who do not wear their hearts on their sleeves. But never, I repeat never, in over seventy years have I witnessed such scenes of joyful welcome as I witnessed in the streets of our capital, as smiling happy faces and uninhibited rapturous applause greeted the Holy Father along the route from the airport to our Youth Rally, from Murrayfield to the historic meeting with the Moderator of the General Assembly of the Church of Scotland, and along the next stage of the ceremonial drive to our Catholic Cathedral. There were tributes all the way — not least from our good friends of the Episcopal Church in Scotland, whose cathedral bellringers welcomed the Holy Father with a quarter-peal of twelve hundred and sixty different changes.

And so it went on, this glad acceptance of the visit of a great leader whose utter sincerity and dedication to the service of God and man had won the affection of so many of our brothers and sisters in Scotland. It was the same story throughout England and Wales. But — I speak as a Scot — nowhere was the reception more vocal, more warm, more enthusiastic than in our lovely land.

Yes — unforgettable days! Thank God for them and for the rekindled sense of mission they have engendered. Now it is all over. Or — is it? Please God we can answer that question with an emphatic 'No'. For months we prepared for the visit of Pope John Paul II in an intensive campaign of prayer and reflection. His promise to visit us launched a programme of spiritual renewal. Despite the anxieties of recent months and weeks, our Vicar of Christ did come to us. We received him with joy — with flag-flying, cheers and applause; with welcoming songs that left us hoarse but happy. Yes, he has come and he has left us inspired and enthused. But now the real work must begin. Now comes the 'follow-up': our enthusiasm must not flag but we must follow up the campaign of spiritual renewal that will change the face of our Church throughout our island home.

Thanks be to God for all that has been achieved. We pray that we may use to the full the graces of this visit. I am the voice of the Catholics of Scotland that joyfully cries out, 'Thank you, John Paul, and God bless you always!'

June 1982

9

THE PAPACY OF JOHN PAUL II

Election as Pope

Cardinal Karol Wojtyla, Archbishop of Cracow in Poland, was elected Bishop of Rome on 16 October 1978, the second day of voting at a conclave of 111 cardinals in the Sistine Chapel in Rome. The news stunned the Roman Catholic Church and the world, for the cardinals had elected the first non-Italian Pope since Adrian VI in the sixteenth century. Cardinal Wojtyla, aged fifty-eight, was the youngest Pope to be elected since Pius IX in 1846; the 264th successor of St Peter and the first from a Communist land, he took the name of John Paul II.

Pope John Paul is the product of a deeply nationalistic Roman Catholic country with a thousand years of tradition, but also with a long experience of partition, invasion, persecution and suffering: even today, Poland is under the grip of martial law. On his election as Pope, Karol Wojtyla had to leave for ever the mountains and lakes of Poland which he knew and loved so well. As he said to a gathering of his countrymen shortly after his election, 'It is not easy to leave my beloved country but if it is the will of God, I must accept it; and I do accept it.'

During his Inaugural Mass in St Peter's Square on 22 October 1978 Pope John Paul said: 'To the See of Peter in Rome there succeeds today a bishop who is not a Roman, a bishop who is the son of Poland. But from this moment he too becomes a Roman. I appeal to all men — pray for me! — help me to be able to serve you! In God's inscrutable providence I have been chosen to continue the mission of Peter and to repeat with similar conviction: "You are the Christ — the Son of the living God".'

From Priest to Pontiff

Karol Wojtyla was ordained priest in 1946 when he was twenty-six years old. He gained a reputation for his brilliant preaching early in his career, and was particularly loved by students and young people. After only twelve years in the ministry he was appointed Auxiliary to the Archbishop of Cracow, whom he succeeded in January 1964. The Second Vatican Council, opened in St Peter's Basilica by Pope John XXIII in October 1962, brought the young bishop to the forefront of Church affairs, and for the next three years he was a frequent contributor to the Council's many debates. At home the Archbishop continued his simple lifestyle and frugal habits. He maintained his interest in young people and continued to go camping, climbing and skiing with them. He was an outspoken and staunch defender of the rights and freedom of individuals, but always looked for dialogue rather than confrontation with the authorities.

On 26 June 1967 Karol Wojtyla was created a Cardinal by Pope Paul VI. Despite his position he was always available to anyone who wanted to see him; he still wore his plain black cassock and his room at the episcopal palace was simple and barely furnished. As a representative of the Polish Bishops' Conference, Cardinal Wojtyla

11

Pope John Paul kisses the ground of England on his arrival at Gatwick Airport, 28 May

took part in all the International Synods of Bishops in Rome, and in 1971 was elected a member of the Synod's permanent Council. The Synod of Bishops was instituted by Pope Paul on 15 September 1965 and was one of the fruits of the Second Vatican Council. Every three years for a period of one month about two hundred bishops from all over the world meet to discuss the most important questions concerning the Church and the world.

Between 1971 and 1978 Cardinal Wojtyla travelled widely, in the United States, the Far East and Europe. In 1976 he was invited by Pope Paul VI to lead the annual Lenten Retreat made by the Pope himself and members of the Vatican Curia. On the evening of 6 August 1978 Pope Paul VI died, at the age of eighty. Cardinal Wojtyla took part in the conclave which elected his successor, Cardinal Albino Luciani, Patriarch of Venice, who took the name John Paul I.

Cardinal Wojtyla had hardly got back to his work in Cracow when on 29 September he received the news of the sudden death of the Pope after only 33 days in office. Less than one month later he himself appeared as Pope John Paul II on the central balcony of St Peter's. Before giving his expected blessing *urbi et orbi* (to the city and the world) in Latin, the new Polish Pope addressed the huge crowd in Italian and immediately won his way into their hearts. He then made his way to the apartment on the top floor of the Apostolic Palace in the Vatican which will be his home for the rest of his life.

A Long Day at the Vatican

The Pope usually begins his day at about 5.30 a.m. He is frequently in his small private chapel in the Apostolic Palace by 6 a.m., where he spends an hour in prayer and meditation before saying Mass. While eating a substantial breakfast the Pope reads the major Italian and international daily newspapers. He works in his study until 11 a.m., writing, dictating and correcting documents and speeches. His output is phenomenal: in 1979, his first full year in office, he is said to have delivered over five hundred addresses.

The rest of the morning is devoted to private audiences with cardinals, bishops, visiting Heads of State, ambassadors, and people from every kind of organisation and walk of life. The Pope often has 'working lunches', and if there are no guests he is joined by his two private secretaries. Lunch is prepared and served by the Polish Sisters who look after the Pope's apartment; it usually takes the form of his favourite Polish dishes, especially when Polish guests are present, although he also eats Italian and other Western food.

Despite his already very long and full day Pope John Paul does not usually take a siesta, preferring instead to relax by walking in the Vatican gardens or up and down the terrace of the Apostolic Palace above his private apartment. Sometimes as he walks on

12

the terrace he recites the Rosary, or reads: he particularly likes books on theology, philosophy and sociology. The Pope is fond of singing and music. He also loves to swim when he can, and has had a swimming pool built at his summer residence of Castelgandolfo, situated in the Alban Hills about fifteen miles outside Rome.

During the afternoon the Pope works in his study for two or three hours. He often continues with private audiences for his advisers or people he was unable to fit in during the morning. He talks with Cardinal Agostino Casaroli, his Secretary of State, and sees the Prefects of the various departments of the Roman Curia who are responsible for the administration of the Roman Catholic Church.

For his dinner the Pope prefers a simple, light meal, especially when he is dining alone or with his secretaries. He may watch the television news while he is eating. He loves meeting people, and on occasion he invites friends to supper at the papal apartments, often joining in a sing-song afterwards. Sometimes he leaves the Vatican to have supper with the staff and students at one of the many training colleges for priests in Rome.

Pope John Paul then spends several more hours working in his study, reading letters and documents sent for his approval and signature. He writes his own letters and spends time preparing himself for the following day. He retires to bed very late, rarely before 1 a.m., having first spent a long period in prayer in his private chapel.

Pastoral Visits Overseas

The Pope has already left the confines of the Vatican and travelled more extensively than any other Pope in history. He has made contact with and spoken to millions of ordinary people, often in their native tongues. On his arrival in Brazil in June 1980 he explained the purpose of his many pastoral visits and missionary pilgramages. 'As Bishop of Rome, the successor of the Apostle Peter, and therefore the Vicar of Christ and the visible Head of His Church, I feel addressed to me the tremendous and comforting command to strengthen my brother bishops in their mission; and with them strengthen the sons of the Catholic Church in a courageous and enlightening faith which will lead them to bear witness before the world to the reasons for their hope in Christ; and to communicate to the world the fathomless riches of Christ's love.'

Pope John Paul II's first overseas visit was in January 1979 to the Dominican Republic and Mexico, where he opened the Third General Conference of Latin American Bishops held at Puebla. His second pastoral visit was to his homeland, Poland, in June of the same year. There in Victory Square, in the heart of Warsaw, he celebrated Mass before hundreds of thousands of Poles. It was an unprecedented event for a Communist country. He visited the concentration camps at Auschwitz which had made such a deep impression on him during his years in Cracow. He called these

Overleaf: **Pope John Paul with the Bishops of England and Wales in Westminster Cathedral, 28 May**

camps, in which four million people died during the Second World War, 'the Golgotha of the modern world'. He visited the bunker in which a Franciscan priest, Blessed Maximilian Kolbe, gave his life to save that of Franciszek Gajowniczek, now 81, the father of a family marked for death. (The Pope is to canonise Blessed Maximilian in October 1982.) His final Mass in Poland was celebrated on the great meadow in the centre of Cracow for two million of his countrymen. John Paul II ended his emotional pilgramage with the words, 'As I depart I kiss the ground, from which my heart can never be detached.'

Also during 1979 the Pope paid a visit to the Republic of Ireland (29 September-1 October). He celebrated Mass for over a million people in Phoenix Park, Dublin; but perhaps the key address of his visit was an impassioned plea for peace at Drogheda, less than thirty miles from the Ulster border. During an hour-long speech to a crowd of over 250,000, including many from Northern Ireland, the Pope said: 'Now I wish to speak to all men and women engaged in violence. I appeal to you, in language of passionate pleading. On my knees I beg you to turn away from the paths of violence and to return to the ways of peace. Further violence in Ireland will only drag down to ruin the land you claim to love and the values you claim to cherish. In the name of God I beg you: return to Christ, who died so that men might live in forgiveness and peace.' Towards the end of his address he proclaimed: 'May no Irish Protestant think that the Pope is an enemy, a danger or a threat. My desire is that instead Protestants would see in me a friend and a brother in Christ.'

The Holy Father then travelled from Ireland to the United States, where on 2 October he delivered an address at the General Assembly of the United Nations in New York. His theme was peace, justice and human rights. In Washington the Pope met President Carter at the White House.

His visit to Turkey later the same year was described by the Pope as the 'first ecumenical voyage' of his Pontificate. He had meetings with Ecumenical Orthodox Patriarch Dimitrios I, and the highlight of the visit was their joint announcement of the establishment of a Catholic-Orthodox Commission to begin a theological dialogue in the quest for unity between the churches.

During 1980 the Pope visited Africa (Zaire, People's Republic of the Congo, Kenya, Ghana, Upper Volta and Ivory Coast); France; Brazil and West Germany. In an address to members of the Council of the Evangelical (Lutheran) Church, the major Protestant church in Germany, the Pope said: 'I recall that in 1510-11 Martin Luther came to Rome as a pilgrim to the tomb of the Prince of the Apostles, but also as a seeker and a questioner. Today I come to you, to the spiritual heirs of Martin Luther. I come as a pilgrim to make through this meeting in a changed world a sign of union in the central mysteries of our faith.'

16

Right and overleaf: **Westminster Cathedral: the Pope and Cardinal Basil Hume receive Holy Communion during Mass**

In 1981 Pope John Paul visited the Philippines and Japan. At the Peace Memorial in Hiroshima, where the world's first nuclear bomb fell on 6 August 1945, he spoke movingly of man's need to learn peaceful means of resolving his conflicts.

The Assassination Attempt on the Pope

This was to be the Pope's last overseas visit for more than a year, for as he was being driven slowly through the huge crowds in St Peter's Square on the afternoon of Wednesday 13 May 1981, at the start of one of his general audiences in Rome, an attempt was made on his life. Two shots, fired at close range, hit him as he stood in the back of his white jeep, leaning over the side to shake hands with pilgrims. The Pope fell back into the arms of his secretary. He was driven at speed back into the Vatican, and minutes later was rushed by ambulance to the Gemelli hospital in Rome. In great pain the Pope received the last rites of the Church, before undergoing five and a half hours of surgery. As news of the attack spread round the world, telegrams expressing shock and sympathy began to pour into the Vatican. In Poland men and women wept openly. 'I pray for that brother who shot me, and whom I have sincerely pardoned,' the Pope told thousands of people who crowded into St Peter's Square on the following Sunday to hear a message recorded at his hospital bedside. 'This shedding of my blood has validated my work,' he said later.

Pope John Paul made a remarkable recovery and was back at his desk again by October, but many people said he was unlikely to leave the Vatican again. Not only has he proved them wrong, he still insists on mingling freely with his flock. In February 1982 he made a visit to Nigeria, the first overseas visit since the attempt on his life. In the northern city of Kaduna the Pope made an appeal to Nigerian Muslims for closer co-operation with Christians. Throughout this visit, his second to Africa, the Holy Father showed remarkable stamina in a region once known as 'the white man's grave' because of the enervating tropical climate. Between 17 and 19 February he also visited the countries of Benin, Gabon and Equatorial Guinea.

In May 1982 the Pope made a four-day pilgrimage to Portugal, to celebrate a Mass of Thanksgiving at the shrine of Our Lady of Fatima. The 65th anniversary of Our Lady's first apparition to the three peasant children on 13 May 1917 was also the first anniversary of the attempt on his life. He told the vast crowds: 'I wanted to express here my gratitude to Our Heavenly Mother for having saved my life.' While at the Marian shrine — on the first evening of his visit there — the Pope was saved from a second assassination attempt.

The Teaching Pope

As head of the Roman Catholic Church Pope John Paul II leads the largest religious body on earth, with over 750 million people — over 18 per cent of the world's population — under his pastoral jurisdiction. So far he has issued three Encyclical Letters during his Pontificate. These are pastoral letters addressed by the Pope to the whole Church. The first, *Redemptor Hominis,* was published in March 1979. It began: 'The redeemer of man, Jesus Christ, is the centre of the universe and of history.' The second Encyclical, *Dives in Misericordia* (Rich in Mercy), was issued at the end of November 1979. In it the Pope showed that the full dignity of man cannot be understood without God the Father, who in his mercy has called man to such a great destiny, revealing his mercy through Christ. *Laborem Exercens* (On Human Work) was issued in September 1981. The Encyclical ends with a reminder from the Pope of the circumstances of its publication: 'I prepared this document for publication on 15 May last, on the ninetieth anniversary of the encyclical *Rerum Novarum* [Pope Leo XIII's 'Workers' Charter'], but it is only after my stay in hospital that I have been able to revise it definitively.'

On 25 October 1979 the Pope issued the Apostolic Exhortation *Catechesi Tradendae.* This document was published as a result of the Fourth General Assembly of the Synod of Bishops held in Rome in 1977 on the theme 'Catechesis in Our Time'.

The first General Assembly convoked by Pope John Paul II met in Rome from 26 September to 25 October 1980. The theme was 'The Role of the Christian Family in the Modern World'. Bishops representing every National Conference throughout the world attended the Assembly, together with observers from various international organisations concerned with the subject of the family. As a result of the Synod the Pope issued an Apostolic Exhortation *Familiaris Consortio* (On Family Life) on 16 December 1981. In it he reaffirms the lifelong commitment of marriage and the teaching of *Humanae Vitae,* the controversial Encyclical issued by Pope Paul VI in 1968 which forbids all forms of artificial contraception.

Looking forward to the Sixth General Assembly of the Synod of Bishops in the autumn of 1983, the Secretary General, Archbishop Jozef Tomko, writes from the Vatican: 'After vast consultation Pope John Paul has chosen "Reconciliation and Penance in the Mission of the Church" as the theme. This is another theme that is fundamental for the Church and the world. Jesus Christ himself began his public ministry with the invitation: "Repent and believe in the Gospel." The Church continues this mission in a world that stands in need of reconciliation, for the world is full of tensions, divisions and lacerations. These latter have their root in the heart of man and in sin. Only by way of a truly deep conversion of the heart and by penance can man, and with him the world, come to reconciliation and peace. The Catholic Church, under the guidance of John Paul II, places itself once more at the heart of the drama of today's man in order to bring him to Christ.'

CHRISTIAN UNITY

A message from Bishop Ramon Torrella, Vice-President of the Vatican Secretariat for Promoting Christian Unity:

The Holy Father's visit to Britain is of great significance at the international as well as at the national level. The Catholic Church is engaged in dialogue with the Orthodox Church, the Anglican Communion, the Methodist, Lutheran and Reformed Churches, and collaborates with the World Council of Churches in many activities. Repaying the visits of successive Archbishops of Canterbury to Rome, the Pope will join in prayer with Archbishop Runcie in Canterbury Cathedral at a time when Anglican-Catholic dialogue has reached an important stage, for both Communions are just beginning their serious study of the work recently concluded by the Anglican-Roman Catholic International Commission.

The Pope is also to meet the Moderator of the General Assembly of the Church of Scotland. This is a reminder that we seek not simply some narrow unity between two Churches but rather to obey Our Lord's will that *all* who believe in him may be one. This obedience calls for all our human efforts, but ultimately it is the work of God the Holy Spirit.

Background

Pope John Paul II is a successor of Simon the Fisherman who was called by Jesus of Nazareth to leave his nets and follow Him, and to become Peter, which means 'Rock'. As leader of the Apostles after the Ascension of Jesus into Heaven, Peter's preaching took him to Rome where he became its first Bishop. In the persecutions under the Emperor Nero, Peter was arrested and condemned to death together with hundreds of other Christians. He was crucified, and his body laid in a cemetery on the Vatican hill.

Christianity continued to spread throughout the known world and at the end of the sixth century Pope Gregory the Great sent St Augustine and forty Roman Benedictine monks to England to preach the Gospel. Having converted King Ethelbert, Augustine became the first Archbishop of Canterbury in the year 597. Since the time of St Peter there has been only one English Pope, Nicholas Breakspear. Originally from St Albans, he became Cardinal Bishop of Ostia, and was elected Pope in 1154. He took the name Adrian IV, and was the first Pope to be called the Vicar of Christ. He never returned to his native England as Pope.

On 31 October 1517, Martin Luther attacked the spiritual authority of the Roman Catholic Church by nailing his ninety-five theses against the Doctrine of Indulgences to the main church door at Wittenberg, the German university town where he was a biblical professor. Luther was not able to compromise with Rome and, in 1521, he was excommunicated. His fateful act had become the catalyst for the Reformation, an historical process with far-reaching consequences for the Christian faith.

Pope John Paul II and Her Majesty The Queen at Buckingham Palace, 28 May

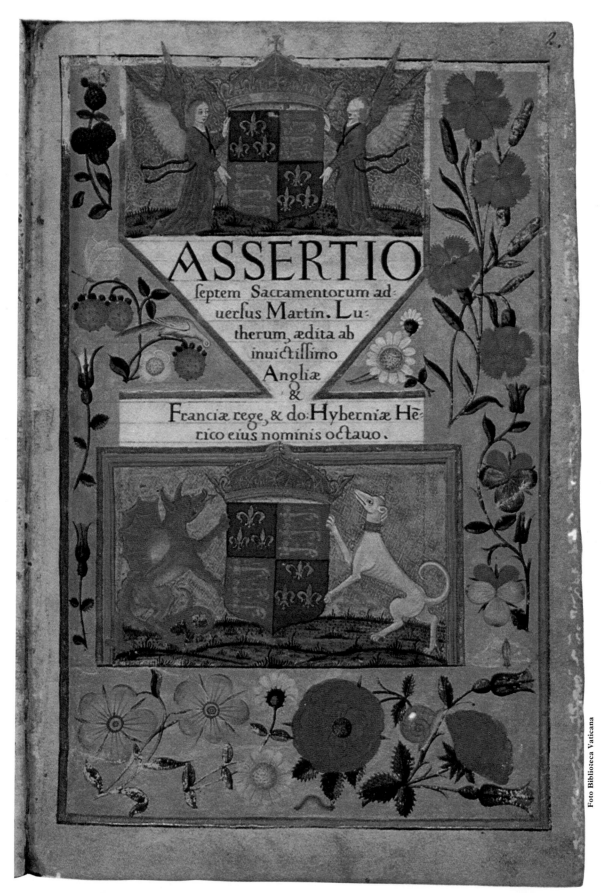

Manuscript copy of Henry VIII's *Assertio Septem Sacramentorum contra Lutherum* presented by Bishop John Clerk to Pope Leo X in 1521, showing the royal arms on the frontispiece

Pope Leo X gave King Henry VIII the title 'Defender of the Faith' for his book against Martin Luther on the Seven Sacraments, *Assertio Septem Sacramentorum contra Lutherum*. The English crown retains this title, which still appears on coins of the realm

cat, gloria turget, ratione friget, feruet inui-
dia. Deniqᵨ, quibus animis aduerfus turchas,
aduerfus faracenos, aduerfus quicquid eft:
ufpiam infidelium confifterent: ijfdem animis confiftant aduerfus unum iftum: uiribus
imbecillum, fed animo, turchis omnibus, o-
mnibus faracenis, omnibus ufᵨ infidelibus
nocentiorem fraterculum ?

Angloru̅ Rex Henricus, Leo decime, mittit

Hoc opus, et fidei tefte̅ et amicitie

H͞ericus

The final page of the manuscript shows a couplet in Henry's own hand:
*Angloru [m] Rex Henricus, Leo decimo, mittit Hoc opus et fidei teste[m] et
amicitie Henricus* (Henry, King of the English, to Leo X, sends this work and
witness of faith and friendship Henry)

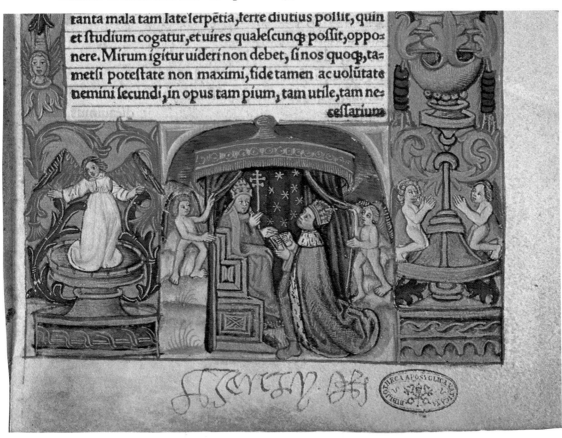

The introductory page of a presentation copy of the printed edition of the
Assertio. The illuminated border symbolises Henry VIII presenting his work
to Pope Leo X. The King's autograph is at the foot of the page

In England, the religious implications of the Reformation were quickly overshadowed by politics. In 1534, Pope Clement VII refused to grant Henry VIII a divorce from Catherine of Aragon. The King responded by rejecting papal authority and promptly declared himself the Head of the Church of England. He then closed all the monasteries and confiscated their land. The boy king Edward VI (1547-53) staunchly upheld the Reformation with the support of the Archbishop of Canterbury, Thomas Cranmer. Queen Mary (1553-58) tried to restore Roman Catholicism in England and had more than two hundred bishops and scholars burnt at the stake for their Protestant faith. Her cousin Reginald Pole became the last Cardinal of Canterbury and Papal Legate of England.

Queen Elizabeth I (1558-1603), however, quickly re-established Protestantism in England. Roman Catholic church leaders were once again replaced by Protestants, the Articles and Prayer Book of Edward VI were restored and the Queen took the title of Supreme Governor of the Church of England. Recalcitrant Roman Catholics were put to death for their faith. In 1570 the Queen was excommunicated by Pope Pius V as a heretic.

A small number of Roman Catholics did succeed in keeping the Faith alive in England, but by the of time the Catholic Emancipation Act of 1829, they constituted only a tiny percentage of the population, located chiefly in the North of England. It was the Great Irish Famine of 1847 which brought the first new wave of Roman Catholics into the cities and towns of Britain. In 1850, Pope Pius IX restored the Roman Catholic Hierarchy of England for the first time since the Reformation. In Scotland it was re-established by Pope Leo XIII in 1878. The faithful gradually increased in number over the years and by May 1982 the Roman Catholic Church in Great Britain represented some six million people.

During this time the 1854 promulgation of the Marian Dogma of the Immaculate Conception by Pope Pius IX; the Decrees on Primacy and Papal Infallibility of the First Vatican Council in 1870; and the 1896 Bull *Apostolicae Curae* of Pope Leo XIII which condemned Anglican orders as 'null and void' set the Roman Catholic and Anglican Churches further apart.

The first steps towards unity were taken when the Second Vatican Council was opened in St Peter's Basilica by Pope John XXIII on 11 October 1962. The first Council of the Church for nearly a century was attended by delegate observers of separated Christian churches. Two years earlier the Pope had established the Vatican Secretariat for promoting Christian unity and on 2 December 1960 he had received Dr Geoffrey Fisher, the 99th Archbishop of Canterbury, at the Vatican. This was the first meeting between the Pope and an Archbishop of Canterbury since the Reformation. It paved the way for John XXIII's successor, Pope Paul VI, and the new

The Pope moves among the sick who filled St George's Cathedral, Southwark, for a special service of anointing, 28 May

Archbishop of Canterbury, Dr Michael Ramsey, to sign a Common Declaration in Rome during 1966. Following the meeting a Joint Preparatory Commission was established, and in October 1969 the Anglican-Roman Catholic International Commission (ARCIC) was appointed. The first *Agreed Statement on Eucharistic Doctrine* was published by the Commission in 1971, followed in 1973 by one on *Ministry and Ordination* and in 1977 another on *Authority in the Church.*

On Whit Sunday 1968 Cardinal John Heenan, Archbishop of Westminster, became the first cardinal to preach at Westminster Abbey since the Reformation. As a gesture of friendship the new Archbishop of Westminster, George Basil Hume, O.S.B., the former Abbot of Ampleforth, was invited to bring his Benedictine monks to sing vespers in Westminster Abbey, after his installation on 25 March 1976. Dr Donald Coggan, the Archbishop of Canterbury, signed a Common Declaration with Pope Paul VI after a service in the Sistine Chapel in April 1977, and in February of the following year Cardinal Hume was invited to address the General Synod of the Church of England.

The Final Report of the Anglican-Roman Catholic International Commission was published in March 1982. The Sacred Congregation for the Doctrine of the Faith in its Observations said: 'The Final Report represents a notable ecumenical endeavour and a useful basis for further steps on the road to reconciliation between the Catholic Church and the Anglican Communion, but does not yet constitute a substantial and explicit agreement on some essential elements of Catholic faith.' Bishops' conferences around the world have been asked by the Vatican Secretariat for Promoting Christian Unity to study and evaluate the Report. The Anglican response is not expected before the 1988 Lambeth Conference.

The views expressed here were given in interviews before the visit of Pope John Paul II to Great Britain. Those interviewed represent the wide range of differing opinion within the churches, and although some admitted to certain reservations all were united in their welcome to the Pope.

The Church of England

When the Archbishop of Canterbury met Pope John Paul II in Accra on 9 May 1980 while they were on separate tours of Africa, Dr Robert Runcie felt that the time had come to invite the Pope to visit Britain. Previous Archbishops had always been to Rome, and it was now thought that the Church of England should return this hospitality. The invitation was officially expressed through the General Synod of the Church of England, when bishops, clergy and laity warmly welcomed the prospect of the visit and expressed their hope that it would be a step forward in the growing relationship between the Anglican and Roman Catholic Churches.

The Most Rev. and Rt Hon. Robert Runcie,
Archbishop of Canterbury:

We are members of the same body, but it is a broken body, and we have to heal
it. We must put an end to the ideas on the one hand that Roman Catholics are
the only Christians, and on the other that the Church was formed again on a
biblical foundation in the sixteenth century, and Roman Catholics are not part of
that Church.

Reconciliation is an important stage on the way to achieving organic unity —
one Christian Church working together despite differences of tradition and even
theological expression. Reconciliation means sinking differences and accepting
each other, accepting one another's Eucharists as true sacraments of Christ's
presence with His people, and recognising each other's ministries as true
ministers of the Gospel. Reconciliation is costly, and pragmatic intercommunion
cannot be a step on the way to achieving a common faith without a consideration
of the unity and doctrine which should underly it. Similarly with ordination: it is
essential to avoid looking at the issues narrowly, in order to create an atmosphere
in which progress can be made. The churches need to achieve the reconciliation
of ministries with something more meaningful than a declaration, but without
the uncomfortable and largely unacceptable task of reordination.

For the Church of England the most difficult aspect hindering full unity with
the Church of Rome is undoubtedly that of jurisdiction. The Anglican principle
of dispersed authority clashes with the primacy of jurisdiction invested in the
Bishop of Rome and presents a major fundamental problem. The Anglican
Communion has always made an important distinction between holding to the
essentials of the Christian faith and allowing for local varieties of theological
expression, liturgical life and cultural customs. Doctrinal agreement between the
churches would need some recognition of this concept of distinguishing between
essentials and non-essentials. Conversely the doctrinal coherence held by the
Roman Catholic Church gives many people the framework of doctrinal and
ethical principles which Anglicanism sometimes finds it difficult to provide.

The Church of England has set out clear stages for study of the ARCIC Final
Report. The matter will be monitored by the Anglican Consultative Council,
who may give a progress report on it, but the final expression of opinion will be
given by the Lambeth Conference in 1988. The General Synod of the Church of
England will have a chance to express its views before the overall
recommendations of the Lambeth Conference. It will be up to the Provinces that
make up the Anglican Communion to translate these recommendations into
practice.

In order to continue the work of ARCIC a new International Commission will be needed, whose first responsibility is to consider the ecclesial implications of the measures of agreement reached by the theologians. The first steps towards this will be taken this year as a result of the papal visit. There ought also to be a pastoral dimension to these new discussions, dealing with such questions as mixed marriages and differing ethical guidance, especially with respect to family planning. The sort of pastoral co-operation which undoubtedly exists in so many places should be encouraged, and the question of joint evangelisation in a multi-faith society must be tackled.

The discussion between the Pope and leaders of British churches at Canterbury marks a very important and significant step forward. It would be wrong to expect too much of such a short meeting, but it will provide an opportunity for the Pope to listen to English Christianity speaking through its own leaders. This is a conversation that will be continued in Rome. In the past the associations have been very much between Anglican leaders and the Pope, two world-wide Christian families talking together, but Anglicans do not comprise the whole of non-Roman Catholic English Christianity. It could improve the unity of Christians in these islands if the Archbishop of Canterbury, as President of the British Council of Churches, is seen to be speaking in concert with other Christian leaders. This meeting will help the Pope to come to a greater knowledge of British Christianity at the present time, and enable him to understand more fully the British expressions of Christianity found in other parts of the world.

It is necessary to look seriously at why certain prejudices exist between churches but also to recognise the danger of being bound by past events. We have to be reconciled in our histories but we certainly must not be locked into our history.

The British Council of Churches
The Rev. Dr Philip Morgan, General Secretary:

Previous church unity negotiations have demonstrated that a relationship of confidence must exist before the hard questions can be asked, and real progress made. My chief hope concerning the papal visit is that it may encourage an atmosphere of confidence enabling us, in due course, to ask the hard questions. There are substantial areas of doctrinal disagreement to be worked through. The Canterbury meeting between the Pope and British church leaders will not be of sufficient length to allow the kind of detailed theological discussion which is necessary to make progress on the large issues affecting unity.

Through the British Council of Churches it has been possible for the member churches to join with the Roman Catholic Church in spiritual preparation for the papal visit. This is something that some member churches acting on their own would not have felt free to do. Dr Morgan feels that it would be 'an enormous gain to the British Council of Churches and to the Roman Catholic Church if she became a member. The British Council of Churches is essentially a meeting place for its 28 member churches. If the Roman Catholic Church joined it would be a different kind of Council, and a good moment to examine the Council's role in the life of the nation.'

The Methodist Church
The Rev. Dr Kenneth G. Greet, Secretary of the Methodist Conference and Moderator of the Free Church Federal Council:

The Methodist Church has the friendliest relations with the Roman Catholic Church at every level. It is involved in bilateral conversations with Rome at both national and international levels. Methodists are committed to the ecumenical movement, and therefore very much hope that the Pope's visit will further the cause of Christian unity. Most Methodists hope that the visit will focus public attention on the Christian religion and that this will give opportunities for all the churches to proclaim their message more effectively.

Dr Greet, who has met Pope John Paul II personally in Rome, looks forward to the private meeting between the Pope and British church leaders at Canterbury. 'He is a warm and engaging personality, though his views on theological and social questions tend to be, in the main, very conservative.'

The Baptist Union of Great Britain and Ireland
The Rev. Dr David S. Russell, General Secretary:

The Baptist Union Council, whilst recognising that considerable differences in faith and practice exist between the Baptist Union and the Roman Catholic Church, nevertheless upholds the right of the Pope to visit his people in this country and wishes to welcome him with Christian courtesy and love. It is our hope that the visit will lead to a greater openness in relations between Catholics and Protestants, a greater readiness to discuss agreements and differences in Christian dialogue, and a greater desire to grow together in our understanding of God's purpose for his Church.

The Baptist Union Council feels that the visit could lead to a realignment of Christian allegiance, resulting in a more marked polarisation than has been evident hitherto, and that this could therefore have a negative effect on the current 'Covenanting for Unity' scheme. For some Baptists the spiritual and pastoral nature of the visit has tended to be blurred by the 'apparent commercialism and financial arrangements'.

The Pope addresses the Bishops of England and Wales, Archbishop's House, Westminster

The United Reformed Church

The Rev. Bernard Thorogood, General Secretary and Clerk of the General Assembly:

The United Reformed Church expressed its view on the papal visit by resolution of the General Assembly, 1981:

The Assembly, disturbed by the publicity given to certain groups of people who have expessed opposition to the coming visit of His Holiness the Pope to Great Britain, and believing that these groups misrepresent the views of the majority in Reformed and Protestant churches, welcomes the Pope's visit. We pray that this may be the occasion of genuine ecumenical encounter, advancing reconciliation and witnessing to our essential unity in Christ Jesus.

In an historic decision on 19 May 1982 the General Assembly of the United Reformed Church narrowly approved the proposals for covenanting between the URC, the Church of England and two other Free Churches.

Canon David Watson, leading Anglican Evangelist:

Much will depend on what the Pope says and does. If he stresses the peculiarly Roman dogmas, the cause for unity will be set right back. He must be, and must be seen to be, thoroughly biblical in all that he says and does.

I personally welcome the visit. I have a deep respect for Pope John Paul and pray that God will use these few days in every way to His glory. Although truth is always important, our attitudes towards one another are even more so — for without love we are nothing. As the Pope visits us, Protestants need to be humble and positive, believing the best, not fearing the worst, and gracious towards a courageous Christian leader.

The Church of Scotland

The Very Rev. Dr William B. Johnston, Convener of the General Assembly's Inter-Church Relations Committee:

The main desire of the Church of Scotland is that the visit should increase the understanding between the churches, promote further inter-church dialogue on the issues that divide, and in particular contribute to better relations between the Protestant and Roman Catholic communities.

The report of the Inter-Church Relations Committee to the 1982 Assembly held in Edinburgh in May stated:

The Committee have accepted gladly the potential for good in the visit but underline strongly also the negative reactions that some may be ready to adopt — the temptation to see in it a challenge to competing loyalty, to magnify the differences in that same competitive spirit, the temptation even to import the conflicts of Ireland. What must be urged, if not a welcome or a dialogue, is the rejection of all aggravation. Silence on such an occasion is not a surrender. It is the quiet assertion of our tradition of generosity and tolerance towards the stranger.

Dr Johnston hopes that the meeting between the Moderator and the Pope will 'lead to greater understanding in the Vatican of the religious situation in Scotland and will be an encouragement to ecumenical conversation between the Church of Scotland and the Roman Catholic Church.' The General Assembly voted in favour of a meeting between the Moderator and the Pope.

The Roman Catholic Church in Scotland

The Rt Rev. Francis Thomson, Bishop of Motherwell and Chairman of the National Commission for Christian Unity of the Bishops' Conference of Scotland:

As a result of the visit of the Holy Father to Scotland, the Roman Catholic Church would hope for a lessening of fear and suspicion and consequently an increase in understanding. A Pope in distant Rome is one thing, even when seen on television, but a Pope who is seen to walk amongst us becomes one to whom people are able more easily to relate. Every person-to-person contact does more for the cause of Christian unity than many sessions of theological discussion. That contact is particularly valuable at the level of the Moderator and the other church leaders.

In a country where a very small but vocal minority have made their opposition to the visit very evident, the most heartening discovery from the aspect of Christian unity has been the welcoming response to the visit by the vast majority. Ordinary people of different religious affiliations and none at all have frequently expressed to their Catholic neighbours their happiness that the Pope should be coming to Scotland.

BACKGROUND TO THE VISIT

The National Pastoral Congress held in Liverpool in May 1980 was one of the most important events for the Roman Catholic Church in England and Wales since the restoration of the Hierarchy in 1850. Attended by over two thousand delegates representing every level of Church life and from all strata of society, it was the most representative gathering of Roman Catholics ever to assemble in England and Wales. The theme of the Congress was 'Jesus Christ, the Way, the Truth, and the Life'; a realistic assessment of the Church's situation in the light of the teachings of the Second Vatican Council was made, and was expressed in the official report, *Liverpool 1980*. In a message to the Congress Pope John Paul said: 'I extend my congratulations for the initiative you are taking in shared responsibility. It is an initiative which bears witness to the variety of gifts in the Body of Christ, and to the vital mission of all baptised persons in the Church who, in union with the hierarchy and under their direction, are building up the Kingdom of God.'

Cardinal Basil Hume, Archbishop of Westminster, and Derek Worlock, Archbishop of Liverpool, Chairman of the Congress Committee, took a copy of *The Easter People*, the response from the Roman Catholic bishops of England and Wales made in the light of the Congress, to Pope John Paul on 23 August 1980, and invited him to visit the Roman Catholic community in England and Wales. Cardinal Gray issued a similar invitation on behalf of Scotland. Eight days later the Vatican announced that the Pope had agreed to make such a visit during the summer of 1982. From the very beginning the Pope had made known the great importance he would attach to the ecumenical aspect of his visit, in the spirit of visits made to Rome by previous Archbishops of Canterbury and by the leaders of other Christian churches in Great Britain.

In the months that followed, preparations for the visit gathered momentum and proposals for an intinerary were made. In England and Wales it was planned that the Pope should visit each of the five Provinces of Westminster, Liverpool, Birmingham, Southwark and Cardiff, and at the seven major venues chosen should celebrate, as far as this was possible, the seven sacraments of the Church. Mgr Ralph Brown was appointed as national co-ordinator of the visit, but each event was autonomous and planned under separate committees. In Scotland a national committee was set up with Father Daniel Hart as executive director, and the theme 'To follow Christ means to say: yes to God, yes to each other, yes to life' was adopted. As part of the preparations the Bishops' Conference of Scotland issued an important statement on *Disarmament and Peace* in March 1982.

During the preparations the Pope announced that diplomatic relations between the Vatican and Great Britain were to be put on a new footing. On 16 January 1982 the Legation of Great Britain to the Holy See was raised to the rank of Embassy, while an Apostolic Nunciature was created in London, with a Pro-Nuncio as Head of Mission. The first Pro-Nuncio is Archbishop Bruno Heim, who had been appointed Apostolic Delegate to Great Britain in 1973.

In his noon Angelus address the following day the Pope spoke about his planned visit to Great Britain. 'May this journey of mine also serve the cause of the rapport between the Catholic Church and the Anglican Communion, and hasten the greatly desired union. For this end, which is of great ecumenical importance, I ask you all for fervent prayers to the Holy Trinity.'

A shadow was cast over the proposed visit when, on 2 April, Argentine forces occupied the Falkland Islands in the South Atlantic. The British Government responded by despatching a large task force to recapture the Islands by force if a settlement could not be reached by diplomatic means. Delivering his Easter Sunday message *urbi et orbi* (to the city and the world) from the central loggia of St Peter's, Pope John Paul said: 'Of late there has been added a grave tension between two countries of Christian tradition, Argentina and Great Britain, involving the loss of human lives and the threat of armed conflict and terrible repercussions in international relations.' The Pope called for immediate negotiations, and there was much speculation in the media about the cancellation of the visit. Speaking at a press conference in London on 19 April Cardinal Hume revealed his own personal fears for the visit: 'I think it would be very difficult indeed for a Pope to go to a country which was at war with another country. He has to be spiritual father of those in both countries, and this would put him in an impossible situation.'

Doubts over the visit continued to grow as the intense diplomatic efforts failed to find a peaceful solution to the conflict. Cardinal Basil Hume, Archbishop of Westminster, and Cardinal Gordon Gray, Archbishop of St Andrews and Edinburgh, were summoned to Rome by the Pope to brief him on the crisis and its possible consequences for his visit to Britain. On their return from Rome they issued a statement which confirmed the Pope's 'profound desire to fulfil the expectations of the Bishops and Catholic community', but warned that further hostilities 'would necessitate a reconsideration of the visit'.

In his noon Regina Caeli message on Sunday 16 May the Pope made his first public statement casting doubt on his visit to Britain. Some Argentine bishops had been openly critical, and it was already clear that by going ahead with his plans the Pope risked alienating the people of Argentina as well as the rest of Latin America, who today comprise nearly half the Catholic population of the world.

The following day the Archbishop of Liverpool, Derek Worlock, who had made friends with the future Pope during the Second Vatican Council, and the Archbishop of Glasgow, Thomas Winning, were sent to Rome in an attempt to avert a last-minute cancellation. At the same time the Archbishop of Canterbury, Dr Robert Runcie, sent a telegram to the Pope suggesting that the cause of Christian unity could suffer a serious setback if he called off his visit.

It seemed as if the Pope was faced with an insoluble dilemma. On 18 May he conferred with Archbishop Alfonso Lopez Trujillo of Medellin, President of the Conference of Latin American Bishops, and the Archbishops from Great Britain. Then, in an unexpected move, the Pope invited the Cardinals of Argentina and Great Britain to Rome to discuss the situation and to celebrate with him a Mass for Peace in St Peter's Basilica. Later Sir Mark Heath, the newly appointed Ambassador to the Holy See, announced that the British Government was prepared to forgo all formal meetings arranged with the Pope to help underline the purely pastoral and ecumenical nature of the visit.

The historic meeting between the four Cardinals and the Pope took place on Friday 21 May, just one week before he was due to arrive in Britain. At 7 a.m. the following morning, 22 May, a unique Mass was celebrated in St Peter's Basilica at the Altar of the Chair. The readings and prayers were said alternately in English and Spanish. Among those concelebrating with the Pope were Cardinals Basil Hume and Gordon Gray from Great Britain, and the Argentinian Cardinals Raul Francisco Primatesta, Archbishop of Cordoba, and Juan Carlos de Aramburu, Archbishop of Buenos Aires. In his address the Pope said: 'We do not ignore the obstacles which at the present moment bar the way to the attainment of a goal which is so essential to the good of the two peoples and to their interests. Yet we reaffirm, with strong faith, our conviction: peace is a duty, peace is possible.' He quoted from St Augustine who once said that the highest title to glory is 'to kill war with the words of negotiation instead of killing men with the sword'.

The Pope, it was learned, had left the final decision on the proposed visit in the hands of British church leaders. On 25 May the Vatican finally confirmed that the visit would go ahead as planned, and at his General Audience in Rome the following day the Pope read the text of a letter he had sent to the Church in Argentina explaining his reasons for the decision. He also announced that he would make a pastoral visit to Argentina, which took place two weeks later and included a meeting with President Galtieri.

On Wednesday 26 May Cardinal Hume stressed the threefold purpose of the Pope's visit: 'Pope John Paul is coming to visit Britain as the Universal Pastor of the Catholic Church. He comes primarily to visit his Roman Catholic people. He comes to preach the gospel of Jesus Christ to them; to share with them in the life of prayer and of the sacraments; to continue that specific task given by Christ to Peter, the first Pope, of "confirming" his brethren in their faith.

'The Holy Father comes to Britain also as a pilgrim of Christian unity. His visit will encourage the continuing work of the churches to achieve the goal of unity.

'Pope John Paul comes to our country as a man of God and an apostle of peace.'

Top: **The Pope and the Archbishop of Canterbury exchange the kiss of peace**
Bottom: **The Pope and the Archbishop of Canterbury kneel together in prayer at the Nave Altar in Canterbury Cathedral**

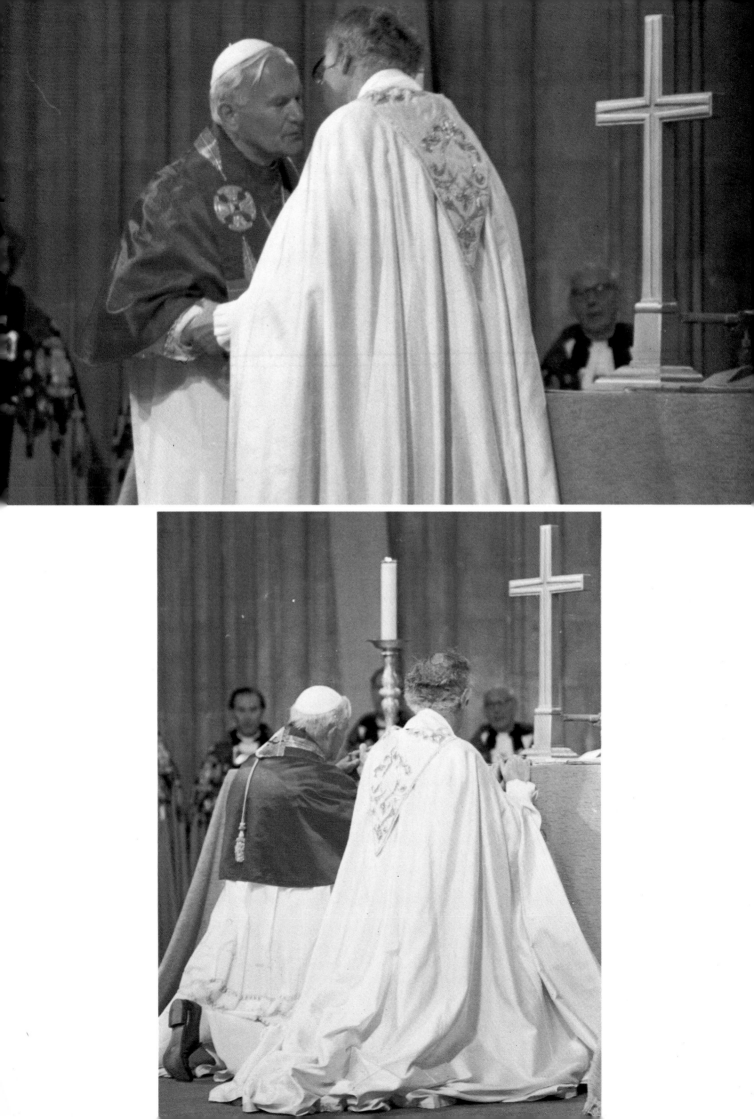

THE PASTORAL VISIT OF POPE JOHN PAUL II TO GREAT BRITAIN

Friday 28 May to Wednesday 2 June 1982

The following extracts from the speeches made by Pope John Paul in the course of his visit to England, Scotland and Wales are given in the chronological order of his pilgrimage.

ENGLAND

ARRIVAL, 28 May

It was just after 8 a.m. on a bright May morning when Pope John Paul alighted at Gatwick Airport from the Alitalia jet which had brought him from Rome for the start of his thirteenth pastoral visit. The Pope's first act on English soil was to kiss the ground. He was welcomed by Cardinal Basil Hume, Archbishop of Westminster, and the Duke of Norfolk on behalf of Her Majesty The Queen.

Cardinal Hume's Address of Welcome

Most Holy Father, I welcome you in the name of the Roman Catholic community of this country and I do so very warmly indeed. We appreciate your presence among us even more deeply because of the many difficulties and uncertainties which have beset the preparation of your visit. . . .

Your visit planned long ago in times of peace now takes place in a time of conflict. . . .

This is a very special moment in our history and in the history of our nation. In your company and with your guidance we now set out together.

The Pope's Reply

Praised be Jesus Christ!

You know that I have come on this pilgrimage of faith in order to make a pastoral visit to the Catholic Church here. Preparations for the journey began a long time ago, and I have been looking forward with joyful anticipation to the opportunity of celebrating the Eucharist and the other sacraments with the Catholic faithful of the local Churches. I am also grateful for the ecumenical encounters which will take place during this journey of faith. The promotion of Christian unity is of great importance, for it corresponds to the will of Our Lord and Saviour Jesus Christ. The sign of unity among all Christians is likewise the way and instrument of effective evangelisation. It is, therefore, my fervent prayer

40

The Pope and the Archbishop of Canterbury give the Blessing at the end of the Celebration of Faith in Canterbury Cathedral, 29 May

that the Lord will bless our efforts to fulfil his will: *ut omnes unum sint* — 'that they may all be one' (John 17:21).

My visit is taking place at a time of tension and anxiety, a time when the attention of the world has been focused on the delicate situation of the conflict in the South Atlantic. . . .

At this moment of history, we stand in urgent need of reconciliation: reconciliation between nations and between peoples of different races and cultures; reconciliation of man within himself and with nature; reconciliation among people of different social conditions and beliefs, reconciliation among Christians. In a world scarred by hatred and injustice and divided by violence and oppression, the Church desires to be a spokesman for the vital task of fostering harmony and unity and of forging new bonds of understanding and brotherhood.

And so I begin my pastoral visit to Britain with the words of Our Lord Jesus Christ: 'Peace be with you'. May the God of peace and reconciliation be with you all. May he bless your families and homes with his deep and abiding peace.

The Pope travelled by special train to Victoria Station, London.

THE SEVEN SACRAMENTS

The theme of the Pope's visit to England and Wales was 'The Seven Sacraments of the Roman Catholic Church'. In a message from the Vatican, Archbishop Luigi Dadaglio, Secretary of the Congregation for the Sacraments and Divine Worship, explains their significance:

The celebration of the Sacraments constitutes a key moment in manifesting the faith of the Christian community and in its growth in faith. Being visible signs of the invisible grace they confer, the Sacraments make us holy and contribute to the building up of the Church, while rendering to God the worship due to him.

Hence the concern of the Second Vatican Council that the sacramental rites take the form of communal celebrations, and express their nature and purpose in a manner that the faithful can more readily comprehend.

MASS AT WESTMINSTER CATHEDRAL, 28 MAY
Baptism

The Pope celebrated the first Mass of his historic visit in Westminster Cathedral, together with the Bishops of England and Wales and visiting Cardinals. Present in the Sanctuary were representatives of the Anglican, Orthodox and Free Churches. In the

43

The Pope and the Archbishop of Canterbury walk past the Paschal Candle to the Chapel of Saints and Martyrs of Our Own Time in Canterbury Cathedral

Overleaf: **Pope John Paul II and Dr Runcie sign the Common Declaration in the Deanery garden at Canterbury, 29 May**

course of the Mass the Pope baptised four people.

> Today, for the first time in history, a Bishop of Rome sets foot on English soil. I am deeply moved at this thought. This fair land, once a distant outpost of the pagan world, has become, through the preaching of the Gospel, a beloved and gifted portion of Christ's vineyard. . . .
>
> I come to confirm the faith of my brother Bishops. I come to remind all believers who today inherit the faith of their fathers that in each diocese the Bishop is the visible sign and source of the Church's unity. I come among you as the visible sign and source of unity for the whole Church. . . .
>
> Christians down the ages often travelled to that city where the Apostles Peter and Paul had died in witness to their faith and were buried. But, during four hundred years, the steady flow of English pilgrims to the tombs of the Apostles shrank to a trickle. Rome and your country were estranged. Now the Bishop of Rome comes to you. I truly come at the service of unity in love, but I come as a friend, too. . . .
>
> I shall administer Baptism here this morning and meditate with you on its meaning. . . .
>
> Through Baptism we are incorporated into Christ. We accept his promise and his commands.
>
> The meaning of Baptism is reflected in the symbolism of the sacramental rite. Water, washing over us, speaks of the redeeming power of Christ's suffering, death and Resurrection, washing away the inheritance of sin, delivering us from a kingdom of darkness into a Kingdom of light and love. By Baptism we are indeed immersed into the death of Christ — baptised, as Saint Paul says, into his death — so as to rise with him in his Resurrection (cf. Romans 6:3-5). The anointing of our heads with oil signifies how we are strengthened in the power of Christ and become living temples of the Holy Spirit. . . .
>
> Through Baptism we are incorporated into the Church. The minister, our parents and godparents sign us with the sign of the Cross, Christ's proud standard. This shows that it is the whole assembly of the faithful, the whole community of Christ, that supports us in the new life of faith and obedience that follows from our Baptism, our new birth in Christ. . . .

Baptism is the foundation of the unity that all Christians have in Christ: a unity we must seek to perfect. When we set out clearly the privilege and the duty of the Christian, we feel ashamed that we have not all been capable of maintaining the full unity of faith and charity that Christ willed for his Church.

> We the baptised have work to do together as brothers and sisters in Christ. The world is in need of Jesus Christ and his Gospel — the Good News that God

Pope John Paul II and Dr Robert Runcie, Archbishop of Canterbury, together with British church leaders after their meeting with the Pope at Canterbury

loves us, that God the Son was born, was crucified and died to save us, that he rose again and that we rose with him, and that in Baptism he has sealed us with the Spirit for the first time, gathered us into a community of love and of witness to his truth. . . .

It is through water and the Holy Spirit that a New People is born, whatever the darkness of the time.

After Mass the Pope went to the Cathedral balcony where he greeted and blessed the large crowds gathered in the piazza below.

MEETING WITH HER MAJESTY THE QUEEN AT BUCKINGHAM PALACE, 28 MAY

After lunch and a short rest in Archbishop's House, Westminster, the Pope was driven through the crowded London streets to Buckingham Palace where he had a short private meeting with Her Majesty The Queen. Then the smaller of the special papal vehicles, one of two used during the visit, drove Pope John Paul through the centre gates of the palace and past the Houses of Parliament and across Westminster Bridge to Southwark.

VISIT TO ST GEORGE'S CATHEDRAL, SOUTHWARK,
Anointing of the Sick, 28 May

Before a moving and simple service the Pope walked slowly among the sick, elderly, handicapped and terminally ill people gathered to receive his blessing. The whole cathedral had been emptied of its pews and transformed into a huge hospital ward. Those on stretchers were accommodated, with their helpers, in the nave, and those in wheelchairs in the aisles. Medical centres were set up around the cathedral, teams of doctors and nurses stood by, and each patient's case-history was recorded in a computer in Archbishop's House in case of emergency. All the sick were anointed, some by the Pope himself.

The Pope gave his address in a specially constructed enclosure outside the cathedral.

My brothers and sisters,

Praised be Jesus Christ! Praised be Jesus Christ who invites us to share in his life through our Baptism. Praised be Jesus Christ who calls us to unite our sufferings to his so that we may be one with him in giving glory to the Father in heaven.

Today I greet you in the name of Jesus. I thank all of you for the welcome you have given me. I want you to know how I have looked forward to this meeting

48

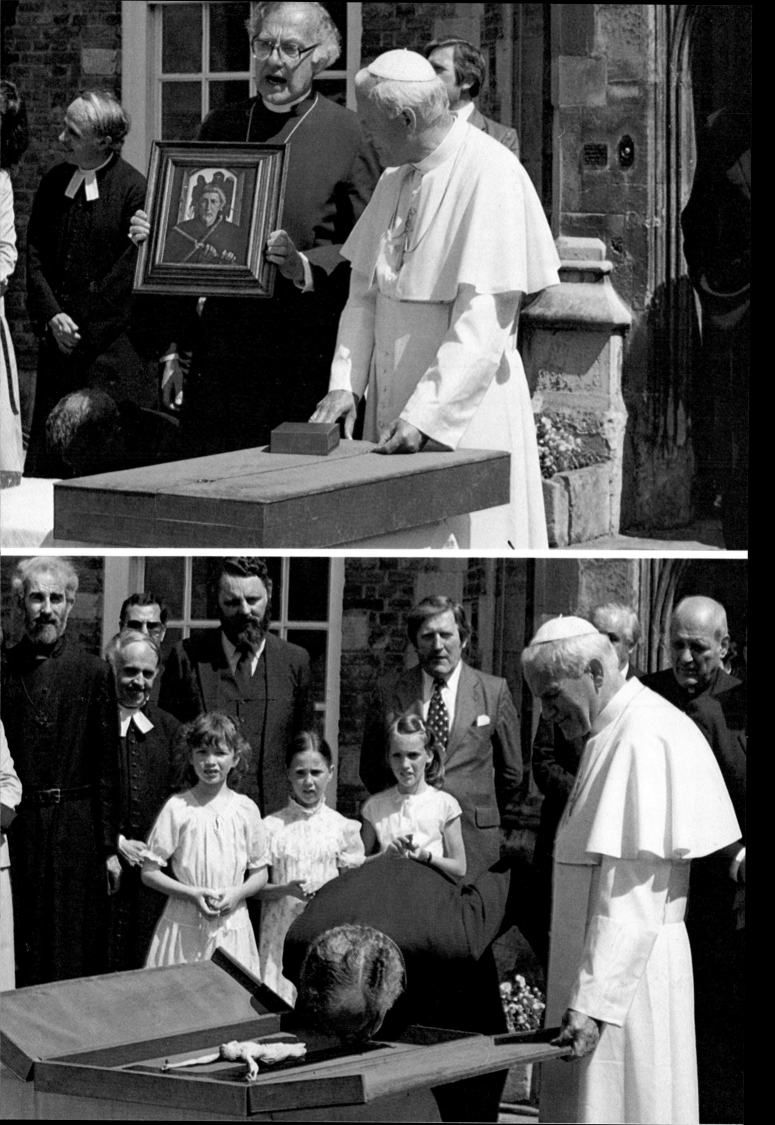

with you, especially with those of you who are sick, disabled or infirm. I myself have had a share in suffering and I have known the physical weakness that comes with injury and sickness.

It is precisely because I have experienced suffering that I am able to affirm with ever greater conviction what Saint Paul says in the second reading: 'Neither death, nor life, nor angels, nor principalities, nor powers, nor things present, nor things to come, nor height, nor depth, nor anything else in all creation, will be able to separate us from the love of God in Christ Jesus our Lord' (Romans 8:38,39).

Dear friends, there is no force or power that can block God's love for you. Sickness and suffering seem to contradict all that is worthy, all that is desired by man. And yet no disease, no injury, no infirmity can ever deprive you of your dignity as children of God, as brothers and sisters of Jesus Christ.

By his dying on the Cross, Christ shows us how to make sense of our suffering. In his Passion we find the inspiration and strength to turn away from any temptation to resentment and grow through pain into new life.

Suffering is an invitation to be more like the Son in doing the Father's will. It offers us an opportunity to imitate Christ who died to redeem mankind from sin. Thus the Father has disposed that suffering can enrich the individual and the whole Church.

We acknowledge that the Anointing of the Sick is for the benefit of the whole person. We find this point demonstrated in the liturgical texts of the sacramental celebration: 'Make this oil a remedy for all who are anointed with it; heal them in body, in soul and in spirit, and deliver them from every affliction.'

The anointing is therefore a source of strength for both the soul and the body. The prayer of the Church asks that sin and the remnants of sin be taken away. It also implores a restoration of health, but always in order that bodily healing may bring greater union with God through the increase of grace.

In her teaching on this sacrament, the Church passes on the truth contained in our first reading from Saint James: 'Is any among you sick? Let him call for the elders of the Church and let them pray over him, anointing him with oil in the name of the Lord; and the prayer of faith will save the sick man, and the Lord will raise him up; and if he has committed sins, he will be forgiven' (James 5:14-15).

This sacrament should be approached in a spirit of great confidence, like the leper in the Gospel that has just been proclaimed. Even the desperateness of the man's condition did not stop him from approaching Jesus with trust. We too must believe in Christ's healing love and reaffirm that nothing will separate us from that love. Surely Jesus wishes to say: 'I will; be clean' (Matthew 8:3); be healed; be strong, be saved.

My dear brothers and sisters, as you live the Passion of Christ you strengthen the Church by the witness of your faith. You proclaim by your patience, your endurance and your joy the mystery of Christ's redeeming power. You will find the crucified Lord in the midst of your sickness and suffering.

As Veronica ministered to Christ on his way to Calvary, so Christians have accepted the care of those in pain and sorrow as privileged opportunities to minister to Christ himself. I commend and bless all those who work for the sick in hospitals, residential homes and centres of care for the dying. I would like to say to you doctors, nurses, chaplains and all other hospital staff: Yours is a noble vocation. Remember it is Christ to whom you minister in the sufferings of your brothers and sisters.

I support with all my heart those who recognise and defend the law of God which governs human life. We must never forget that every person, from the moment of conception to the last breath, is a unique child of God and has a right to life. This right should be defended by the attentive care of the medical and nursing professions and by the protection of the law. Every human life is willed by our heavenly Father and is a part of his loving plan.

No state has the right to contradict moral values which are rooted in the nature of man himself. These values are the precious heritage of civilisation. If society begins to deny the worth of any individual or to subordinate the human person to pragmatic or utilitarian considerations, it begins to destroy the defences that safeguard its own fundamental values.

Today I make an urgent plea to this nation. Do not neglect your sick and elderly. Do not turn away from the handicapped and the dying. Do not push them to the margins of society. For if you do, you will fail to understand that they represent an important truth. The sick, the elderly, the handicapped and the dying teach us that weakness is a creative part of human living, and that suffering can be embraced with no loss of dignity. Without the presence of these people in your midst you might be tempted to think of health, strength and power as the only important values to be pursued in life. But the wisdom of Christ and the power of Christ are to be seen in the weakness of those who share his sufferings.

Let us keep the sick and the handicapped at the centre of our lives. Let us treasure them and recognise with gratitude the debt we owe them. We begin by imagining that we are giving to them; we end by realising that they have enriched us.

Overleaf: **Wembley Stadium decked in the papal colours for the celebration of Mass, 29 May**

> May God bless and comfort all who suffer. And may Jesus Christ, the Saviour
> of the world and healer of the sick, make his light shine through human weakness
> as a beacon for us and for all mankind. Amen.

The Pope returned to Archbishop's House, Westminster, where he addressed the Bishops of England and Wales before proceeding to the Pro-Nunciature in Wimbledon. He spent his first two nights in England as the guest of the Pro-Nuncio, Archbishop Bruno Heim.

MEETING WITH RELIGIOUS, DIGBY STUART COLLEGE, ROEHAMPTON, 29 MAY

The Pope left the Pro-Nunciature early on Saturday morning and addressed 4,500 religious at Digby Stuart Training College in South London. Some of the contemplatives had not been out of their enclosures for many years. Those present represented 17,000 Catholic and 2,000 Anglican religious, priests, brothers and sisters. Before they renewed their vows in his presence the Pope addressed them:

> To most people you are known for what you do. Visitors to your abbeys and religious houses see you celebrate the liturgy, or follow you in prayer and contemplation. People of all ages and conditions benefit directly from your many different services to ecclesial and civil society. You teach; you care for the sick; you look after the poor, the old, the handicapped; you bring the word of God to those near and far; you lead the young to human and Christian maturity.
>
> Most people know what you do, and admire and appreciate you for it. Your true greatness, though, comes from what you are. Perhaps what you are is less known and understood. In fact, what you are can only be grasped in the light of the 'newness of life' revealed by the Risen Lord. In Christ you are a 'new creation' (cf. 2 Corinthians 5:17).

Pope John Paul left by helicopter for Canterbury where he had an informal meeting with Prince Charles in the Deanery before taking part in a Celebration of Faith in the Cathedral Church of Christ, Canterbury.

CANTERBURY CATHEDRAL, 29 MAY
A Celebration of Faith

This special service held in Canterbury Cathedral is of immense significance for all Christians in England. Pope John Paul II and the Archbishop of Canterbury, Dr Robert Runcie, Primate of the Anglican Communion, entered the mother church of the Anglican Communion by the west door. On reaching the Nave Altar they knelt together in silent prayer before greeting each other with a kiss of peace. The

The Pope at the door of the helicopter which took him to many of the places he visited during his demanding tour of Britain

Archbishop welcomed the Pope on his pilgrimage to Canterbury in the following address:

This is a service of celebration, but the present moment is full of pain for so many in the world.

Millions are hungry and the sacred gift of life is counted cheap while the nations of the world use some of their best resources and much of their precious store of human ingenuity in refining weapons of death.

With so much to celebrate in life and so much work to be done to combat life's enemies, disease and ignorance, energy is being wasted in conflict. Our minds inevitably turn to the conflict and the tragic loss of life in the South Atlantic, and we also remember the sufferings of Your Holiness's own fellow countrymen in Poland.

But Christians do not accept hunger, disease and war as inevitable. The present moment is not empty of hope, but waits to be transformed by the power which comes from remembering our beginnings and by the power which comes from a lively vision of the future.

Remembering our beginnings: celebrating our hope for the future: freeing ourselves from cynicism and despair in order to act in the present: it is this style of Christian living which gives shape to this service.

Every Christian service contains this element of remembering the beginnings of our community, when Our Lord walked this earth. At this season of the year, we particularly remember the gift of the Holy Spirit at the first Pentecost and the sending out of the Apostles to carry the faith of Jesus Christ to the furthest ends of the world. We recall one of the first missionary endeavours of the Roman Church, in its efforts to recapture for Christ a Europe overwhelmed by the barbarians. In the year 597, in the words of the English historian, the Venerable Bede, Your Holiness's great predecessor Gregory, 'prompted by divine inspiration, sent a servant of God named Augustine and several more God-fearing monks with him to preach the word of God to the English race.' Augustine became the first Archbishop of Canterbury, and I rejoice that the successors of Gregory and Augustine stand here today in the church which is built on their partnership in the Gospel.

We shall trace and celebrate our beginnings in this service by reaffirming our baptismal vows made at the font at the beginning of Christian life and by saying together the creed, an expression of the heart of our common Christian faith, composed in the era before our unhappy division.

The emphasis, then, will be on the riches of what we share and upon the existing unity of the Christian Church, which transcends all the political

The Pope kisses a young child at Coventry Airport while the Most Rev. Maurice Couve de Murville, Archbishop of Birmingham, looks on

divisions and frontiers imposed upon the human family. One of the gifts Christians have to make to the peace of the world is to live out the unity that has already been given to them in their common love of Christ.

But our unity is not in the past only, but also in the future. We have a common vision, which also breaks up the lazy prejudices and easy assumptions of the present. The Chapel of the Martyrs of the twentieth century is the focus for our celebration of a common vision. We believe even in a world like ours which exalts and applauds self-interest and derides self-sacrifice, that 'the blood of the martyrs shall create the holy places' of the earth. Our own century has seen the creation of ruthless tyrannies by the use of violence and of cynical disregard of truth. We believe that such empires, founded on force and lies, destroy themselves. The kingdom spoken of by Our Lord Jesus Christ is built by self-sacrificing love which can even turn places of horror and suffering into signs of hope. We think of Your Holiness's own fellow countryman, the priest Maximilian Kolbe, who died in place of another in the hell of Auschwitz. We remember with gratitude our own brother, Archbishop Janani Luwum of Uganda, who worked in the worst conditions for Christ's kingdom of love and justice and whose death inspires us still and will mark the future more deeply than the lives of the oppressors.

We remember all the martyrs of our century of martyrs, who have confirmed Christ's Church in the conviction that even in the places of horror, the concentration camps and prisons and slums of our world — nothing in all creation can separate us from the active and creative love of God in Jesus Christ Our Lord.

If we remember that beginning in Jesus Christ Our Lord, if we can face the suffering involved in travelling his way, if we can lift our eyes beyond the historic quarrels which have tragically disfigured Christ's Church and wasted so much Christian energy, then we shall indeed enter a faith worthy of celebration, because it is able to remake our world.

From the welcome, the service moved to a celebration of common faith at the High Altar. The Pope and the Archbishop kissed the Canterbury Gospels, a gift from Pope St Gregory the Great to St Augustine, and they were placed symbolically on the throne of St Augustine.

In his address the Pope said:

The passages which Archbishop Runcie and I have just read are taken from the Gospel according to John and contain the words of our Lord Jesus Christ on the eve of his Passion. While he was at supper with his disciples, he prayed 'that they may all be one; even as thou, Father, art in me, and I in thee, that they also

Pope John Paul greets the huge crowd who gathered for the Mass of Pentecost at Coventry Airport, 30 May

Overleaf: **Young people interpret the Scripture reading for the Mass**

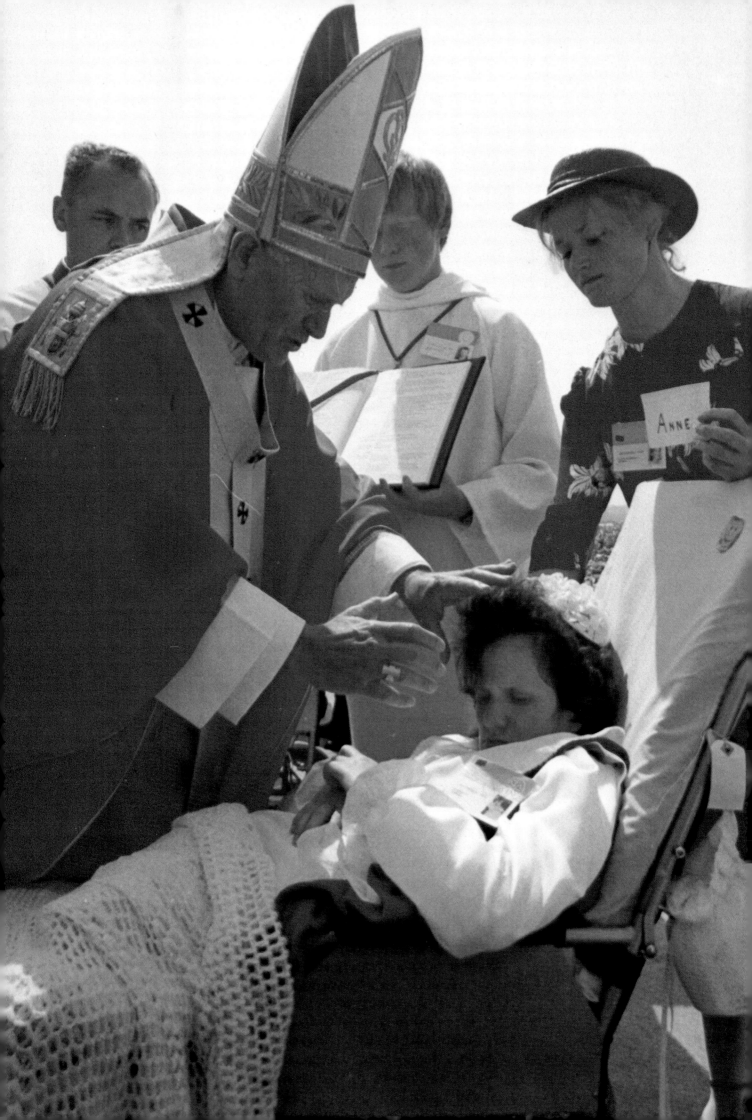

may be in us, so that the world may believe that thou hast sent me' (John 17:21). . . .

Christ's words resound in a special way today in this hallowed Cathedral which recalls the figure of the great missionary Saint Augustine whom Pope Gregory the Great sent forth so that through his words the sons and daughters of England might believe in Christ.

Dear brethren, all of us have become particularly sensitive to these words of the priestly prayer of Christ. The Church of our time is the Church which participates in a particular way in the prayer of Christ for unity and which seeks the ways of unity, obedient to the Spirit who speaks in the words of the Lord. We desire to be obedient, especially today, on this historic day which centuries and generations have awaited. We desire to be obedient to him whom Christ calls the Spirit of truth. . . .

In a few moments we shall renew our baptismal vows together. We intend to perform this ritual, which we share in common as Anglicans and Catholics, as a clear testimony to the one sacrament of Baptism by which we have been joined to Christ. At the same time we are humbly mindful that the faith of the Church to which we appeal is not without the marks of our separation. Together we shall renew our renunciation of sin in order to make it clear that we believe that Jesus Christ has overcome the powerful hold of Satan upon 'the world' (John 14:17). We shall profess anew our intention to turn away from all that is evil and to turn towards God who is the author of all that is good and the source of all that is holy. . . . In this way the renewal of our baptismal vows will become a pledge to do all in our power to co-operate with the grace of the Holy Spirit, who alone can lead us to the day when we will profess the fullness of our faith together.

We can be confident in addressing our prayer for unity to the Holy Spirit today, for according to Christ's promise the Spirit, the Counsellor, will be with us for ever (cf. John 14:16). It was with confidence that Archbishop Fisher made bold to visit Pope John XXIII at the time of the Second Vatican Council, and that Archbishops Ramsey and Coggan came to visit Pope Paul VI. It is with no less confidence that I have responded to the promptings of the Holy Spirit to be with you today at Canterbury.

My dear brothers and sisters of the Anglican Communion, 'whom I love and long for' (Philippians 4:1), how happy I am to be able to speak directly to you today in this great Cathedral! The building itself is an eloquent witness both to our long years of common inheritance and to the sad years of division that followed. Beneath this roof Saint Thomas Becket suffered martyrdom. Here too

One of the young people who received the Sacrament of Confirmation at Coventry Airport on Pentecost Sunday, 30 May

Overleaf: **The Most Rev. Derek Worlock, Archbishop of Liverpool, with the Pope and Cardinal Basil Hume in Liverpool**

we recall Augustine and Dunstan and Anselm and all those monks who gave such diligent service in this church. The great events of salvation history are retold in the ancient stained glass windows above us. And we have venerated here the manuscript of the Gospels sent from Rome to Canterbury thirteen hundred years ago. Encouraged by the witness of so many who have professed their faith in Jesus Christ through the centuries — often at the cost of their own lives — a sacrifice which even today is asked of not a few, as the new chapel we shall visit reminds us — I appeal to you in this holy place, all my fellow Christians, and especially the members of the Church of England and the members of the Anglican Communion throughout the world, to accept the commitment to which Archbishop Runcie and I pledge ourselves anew before you today. This commitment is that of praying and working for reconciliation and ecclesial unity according to the mind and heart of our Saviour Jesus Christ.

On this first visit of a Pope to Canterbury, I come to you in love — the love of Peter to whom the Lord said, 'I have prayed for you that your faith may not fail; and when you have turned again, strengthen your brethren' (Luke 22:32). I come to you also in the love of Gregory, who sent Saint Augustine to this place to give the Lord's flock a shepherd's care (cf.1 Peter 5:2). Just as every minister of the Gospel must do, so today I echo the words of the Master: 'I am among you as one who serves' (Luke 22:27). With me I bring to you, beloved brothers and sisters of the Anglican Communion, the hopes and the desires, the prayers and good will of all who are united with the Church of Rome, which from earliest times was said to 'preside in love'.

Archbishop Runcie will join me in signing a Common Declaration, in which we give recognition to the steps we have already taken along the path of unity, and state the plans we propose and the hopes we entertain for the next stage of our common pilgrimage. And yet these hopes and plans will come to nothing if our striving for unity is not rooted in our union with God. . . . May the dialogue we have begun lead us to the day of full restoration of unity in faith and love.

Towards the end of the service the Pope and the Archbishop, together with other church representatives, each placed a lighted candle in a seven-branched candlestick in the Chapel of Saints and Martyrs of Our Own Time. The martyrs named were:

Maximilian Kolbe, a Polish priest who in the Second World War took the place of a fellow prisoner at Auschwitz who was going to the gas chamber;

Dietrich Bonhoeffer, the eminent German Lutheran pastor and theologian who was put to death in a concentration camp shortly before the end of the Second World War;

Janani Luwum, Archbishop of Uganda, who was tortured and killed during Idi Amin's reign of terror;

67

Top: **The Most Rev. Derek Worlock, Archbishop of Liverpool, with the Pope in Liverpool**

Bottom: **Young people of Toxteth give the Pope an enthusiastic welcome**

Maria Skobtsova, a Russian Orthodox nun from the Ukraine, martyred in the Second World War;

Martin Luther King, the black American Baptist minister assassinated in 1968;

Oscar Romero, the Archbishop of San Salvador, murdered while saying Mass in March 1980;

The Unknown Martyrs of Our Own Time.

The Archbishop and the Pope gave the blessing together before kneeling in prayer at the site of the martyrdom of St Thomas Becket, the Archbishop of Canterbury murdered by knights of King Henry II on 29 December 1170.

COMMON DECLARATION OF POPE JOHN PAUL II AND THE ARCHBISHOP OF CANTERBURY,
(Signed in the Deanery Garden, Canterbury, 29 May 1982)

In the Cathedral Church of Christ at Canterbury the Pope and the Archbishop of Canterbury have met on the eve of Pentecost to offer thanks to God for the progress that has been made in the work of reconciliation between our Communions. Together with leaders of other Christian Churches and Communities we have listened to the Word of God; together we have recalled our one baptism and renewed the promises then made; together we have acknowledged the witness given by those whose faith has led them to surrender the precious gift of life itself in the service of others, both in the past and in modern times.

The bond of our common baptism into Christ led our predecessors to inaugurate a serious dialogue between our Churches, a dialogue founded on the Gospels and the ancient common traditions, a dialogue which has as its goal the unity for which Christ prayed to his Father 'so that the world may know that thou has sent me and hast loved them even as thou hast loved me' (John 17:23). In 1966, our predecessors Pope Paul VI and Archbishop Michael Ramsey made a Common Declaration announcing their intention to inaugurate a serious dialogue between the Roman Catholic Church and the Anglican Communion which would 'include not only theological matters such as Scripture, Tradition and Liturgy, but also matters of practical difficulty felt on either side'. After this dialogue had already produced three statements on Eucharist, Ministry and Ordination, and Authority in the Church, Pope Paul VI and Archbishop Donald Coggan, in their Common Declaration in 1977, took the occasion to encourage the completion of the dialogue on these three important questions so that the

Right: **Huge crowds welcome the Pope outside the Metropolitan Cathedral of Christ the King, Liverpool, 30 May**

Overleaf: **Inside the Metropolitan Cathedral, Liverpool, during Mass on the evening of Pentecost**

Commission's conclusions might be evaluated by the respective authorities through procedures appropriate to each Communion. The Anglican-Roman Catholic International Commission has now completed the task assigned to it with the publication of its Final Report, and as our two Communions proceed with the necessary evaluation, we join in thanking the members of the Commission for their dedication, scholarship and integrity in a long and demanding task undertaken for love of Christ and for the unity of his Church.

The completion of this Commission's work bids us look to the next stage of our common pilgrimage in faith and hope towards the unity for which we long. We are agreed that it is now time to set up a new international Commission. Its task will be to continue the work already begun: to examine, especially in the light of our respective judgements on the Final Report, the outstanding doctrinal differences which still separate us, with a view towards their eventual resolution; to study all that hinders the mutual recognition of the ministries of our Communions; and to recommend what practical steps will be necessary when, on the basis of our unity in faith, we are able to proceed to the restoration of full communion. We are well aware that this new Commission's task will not be easy, but we are encouraged by our reliance on the grace of God and by all that we have seen of the power of that grace in the ecumenical movement of our time.

While this necessary work of theological clarification continues, it must be accompanied by the zealous work and fervent prayer of Roman Catholics and Anglicans throughout the world as they seek to grow in mutual understanding, fraternal love and common witness to the Gospel. Once more, then, we call on the bishops, clergy and faithful people of both our Communions in every country, diocese and parish in which our faithful live side by side. We urge them all to pray for this work and to adopt every possible means of furthering it through their collaboration in deepening their allegiance to Christ and in witnessing to him before the world. Only by such collaboration and prayer can the memory of the past enmities be healed and our past antagonisms overcome.

Our aim is not limited to the union of our two Communions alone, to the exclusion of other Christians, but rather extends to the fulfilment of God's will for the visible unity of all his people. Both in our present dialogue, and in those engaged in by other Christians among themselves and with us, we recognise in the agreements we are able to reach, as well as in the difficulties which we encounter, a renewed challenge to abandon ourselves completely to the truth of the Gospel. Hence we are happy to make this Declaration today in the welcome presence of so many fellow Christians whose Churches and Communities are already partners with us in prayer and work for the unity of all.

With them we wish to serve the cause of peace, of human freedom and human dignity, so that God may indeed be glorified in all his creatures. With them we greet in the name of God all men of good will, both those who believe in him and those who are still searching for him.

This holy place reminds us of the vision of Pope Gregory in sending St Augustine as an apostle to England, full of zeal for the preaching of the Gospel and the shepherding of the flock. On this eve of Pentecost, we turn again in prayer to Jesus, the Good Shepherd, who promised to ask the Father to give us another Advocate to be with us for ever, the Spirit of truth (cf. John 14:16), to lead us to the full unity to which he calls us. Confident in the power of this same Holy Spirit, we commit ourselves anew to the task of working for unity with firm faith, renewed hope and ever deeper love.

CONVERSATION WITH CHURCH LEADERS, 29 MAY

When the service was over the Pope joined in a unique conversation with British church leaders drawn together by the British Council of Churches, in the home of the Dean of Canterbury. Those taking part were:

Geoffrey Bowes, Recording Clerk of the Religious Society of Friends;

Robert Caffyn, Treasurer of the British Council of Churches;

The Rev. Dr Kenneth Greet, Secretary to the Methodist Conference and Moderator of the Free Church Federal Council;

The Most Rev. Alastair Haggart, Primus of the Scottish Episcopal Church, Chairman of the British Council of Churches Division of Ecumenical Affairs;

The Rt Rev. W.B. Johnston, Former Moderator of the Church of Scotland, Chairman of the British Council of Churches Executive;

Archbishop Methodios of Thyateira, Metropolitan of the Greek Orthodox Church in Great Britain;

Dame Diana Reader-Harris, President of the Church Missionary Society, Chairman of Christian Aid;

The Rev. Dr David Russell, General Secretary, Baptist Union of Great Britain and Ireland;

The Rev. Bernard Thorogood, General Secretary, United Reformed Church;

The Rev. Jeremiah McIntyre, Overseer of the New Testament Church of God;

The Most Rev. Gwilym Williams, Archbishop of Wales;

The Rev. Dr Philip Morgan, General Secretary of the British Council of Churches.

After listening to short prepared addresses by the Rev. Dr Philip Morgan, the Most Rev. Alastair Haggart and the Rev. Dr Kenneth Greet, the Pope said in the course of his formal speech:

73

By baptism and the degree of common faith we have just been celebrating in the Cathedral, [the Lord] has already established between us a certain communion, a communion that is real even if it is limited. . . .

But such communion in the Spirit cannot and must not remain something abstract. It has to find expression in the life of our Churches and Communities; it has to be sufficiently visible to be even now a witness we give together to our will for Christian unity in a world that is so sadly divided, a world in which peace is imperilled from so many sides. For these reasons it is a joy for me to hear from you of your hopes for the growth of Christians in these countries into deeper communion, a growth to which through God's grace we are all committed, a growth which we all intend to foster whatever the difficulties we may experience. I have been so happy to learn of the co-operation of the Catholic Church not only with individual Churches and Communities but also with many of the initiatives of the British Council of Churches. I am also pleased to know of the relations of confidence between the Catholic Bishops and the leaders of other Churches and Communities which do so much to facilitate co-operation in evangelisation in those areas in which this is already possible.

You have spoken to me frankly of your hopes and of your problems. Clearly in a short and informal meeting like this we cannot discuss everything. It is my hope, and I am sure it is also yours, that our meeting this morning will not be the end of this fruitful exchange but rather a beginning. I would like to think that, before too long, some of you would be prepared to visit Rome together with some representatives of the Episcopal Conferences of Great Britain and to have further conversations with the Secretariat for Promoting Christian Unity and other offices of the Roman Curia. Thus, please God, we should be able to build further on the foundations so happily laid today. . . .

. . . the Pope longs for the day when, in fulfilment of Christ's will, we shall all be one — one with him and one with each other. God grant that that day may not be long delayed.

After an exchange of gifts with the Archbishop, the Pope left Canterbury by helicopter for Wembley.

THE FIRST MASS OF PENTECOST, WEMBLEY STADIUM, 29 MAY

Over 80,000 people attended the first Mass of Pentecost celebrated by the Pope in Wembley Stadium, which Cardinal Hume described as having been turned into a parish church for the occasion. The Pope's arrival was greeted with the singing of 'Come Holy Ghost, Creator, Come'.

Archbishop Paul Marcinkus, Head of the Vatican Bank and personal bodyguard to Pope John Paul during his overseas visits

As I look at this great assembly I am full of respect for each of you. You are God's sons and daughters; he loves you. I believe in you. I believe in all mankind. I believe in the unique dignity of every human being. I believe that each individual has a value that can never be ignored or taken away.

Yet I also know that often, too often, human dignity and human rights are not respected. Man is set against man, class against class, in useless conflicts. Immigrants, people of a different colour, religion or culture suffer discrimination and hostility. The heart of man is restless and troubled. Man conquers space but is unsure about himself; he is confused about the direction in which he is heading. It is tragic that our technological mastery is greater than our wisdom about ourselves. All this must be changed. 'O Lord, the earth is full of your creatures . . . When you send forth your Spirit, they are created, and you renew the face of the earth' (Psalms 104:24,30). Let this be our plea. May we be renewed in the depths of our hearts in the power of the Holy Spirit.

Together we shall renew our baptismal promises. We shall reject sin, and the glamour of evil, and Satan, the father of sin and prince of darkness. We shall profess our faith in the One God, in his Son, our Saviour Jesus Christ, in the coming of the Holy Spirit, in the Church, in life everlasting. And we shall be responsible for the words we say, and be bound by an alliance with our God. . . .

Let us learn this from Mary our Mother. In England, 'the Dowry of Mary', the faithful, for centuries have made pilgrimage to her shrine at Walsingham. Today Walsingham comes to Wembley, and the statue of Our Lady of Walsingham, present here, lifts our minds to meditate on our Mother. She obeyed the will of God fearlessly and gave birth to the Son of God by the power of the Holy Spirit. Faithful at the foot of the Cross, she then waited in prayer for the Holy Spirit to descend on the infant Church. It is Mary who will teach us how to be silent, how to listen for the voice of God in the midst of a busy and noisy world. It is Mary who will help us to find time for prayer. Through the Rosary, that great Gospel prayer, she will help us to know Christ. We need to live as she did, in the presence of God, raising our minds and hearts to him in our daily activities and worries.

May your homes become schools of prayer for both parents and children. God should be the living heart of your family life. Keep Sunday holy. Go to Mass every Sunday. At Mass the People of God gather together in unity around the altar to worship and to intercede. At Mass you exercise the great privilege of your Baptism: to praise God in union with Christ his Son; to praise God in union with his Church.

76

MEETING WITH POLISH COMMUNITY, PENTECOST SUNDAY, 30 MAY

Early in the morning on Pentecost Sunday the Pope went to the Crystal Palace National Sports Centre in South London to meet 24,000 of his fellow countrymen. Britain is home to 150,000 Polish expatriates, most of whom arrived during the Second World War. Deeply moved by the occasion, the Pope gave an hour-long address in his native tongue. He spoke to the Poles not as emigrants, but rather as 'Poland torn away from her own frontiers', and he went on to say that 'What today we have become accustomed to calling "Poland in Britain" was formed as the very backbone of Poland, fighting for the sacred cause of her independence.'

MASS AT COVENTRY AIRPORT, 30 MAY
Confirmation

On a gloriously sunny morning Pope John Paul celebrated the Mass of Pentecost at Coventry Airport for a crowd of 350,000 people, the largest of any gathering during his visit to Britain. On his arrival at the airport the Pope was driven among the people in his large papal vehicle.

We are close to the city of Coventry, a city devastated by war but rebuilt in hope. The ruins of the old Cathedral and the building of the new are recognised throughout the world as a symbol of Christian reconciliation and peace. . . .

Our world is disfigured by war and violence. The ruins of the old Cathedral constantly remind our society of its capacity to destroy. And today that capacity is greater than ever. People are having to live under the shadow of a nuclear nightmare. Yet people everywhere long for peace. . . .

What is this peace for which we long? What is this peace symbolised by the new Cathedral of Coventry? Peace is not just the absence of war. It involves mutual respect and confidence between peoples and nations. It involves collaboration and binding agreements. Like a cathedral, peace has to be constructed, patiently and with unshakeable faith.

Wherever the strong exploit the weak, wherever the rich take advantage of the poor, wherever great powers seek to dominate and to impose ideologies, there the work of making peace is undone; there the cathedral of peace is again destroyed. Today, the scale and the horror of modern warfare — whether nuclear or not — makes it totally unacceptable as a means of settling differences between nations. War should belong to the tragic past, to history; it should find no place on humanity's agenda for the future.

And so, this morning, I invite you to pray with me for the cause of peace. Let

Overleaf: **The Pope kisses a young child on his arrival at Manchester. With him is the Rt Rev. Thomas Holland, Bishop of Salford**

us pray earnestly for the Special Session of the United Nations on Disarmament which begins soon. The voices of Christians join with others in urging the leaders of the world to abandon confrontation and to turn their backs on policies which require the nations to spend vast sums of money for weapons of mass destruction. We pray this Pentecost that the Holy Spirit may inspire the leaders of the world to engage in fruitful dialogue. May the Holy Spirit lead them to adopt peaceful ways of safeguarding liberty which do not involve the threat of nuclear disaster. Yet the cathedral of peace is built of many small stones. Each person has to become a stone in that beautiful edifice. All people must deliberately and resolutely commit themselves to the pursuits of peace. Mistrust and division between nations begin in the heart of individuals. . . .

I would now like to speak especially to the young people who are about to receive the Sacrament of Confirmation. . . .

Christ's gift of the Holy Spirit is going to be poured out upon you in a particular way. You will hear the words of the Church spoken over you, calling upon the Holy Spirit to confirm your faith, to seal you in his love, to strengthen you for his service. You will then take your place among fellow-Christians throughout the world, full citizens now of the People of God. You will witness to the truth of the Gospel in the name of Jesus Christ. You will live your lives in such a way as to make holy all human life. Together with all the confirmed, you will become living stones in the cathedral of peace. Indeed you are called by God to be instruments of his peace. . . .

[The Pope went on to mention Cardinal Newman (1801-90). A leader of the Oxford Movement and the most outstanding Anglican of his day, Newman was received into the Roman Catholic Church in 1845, and through his preaching and numerous writings has had a profound and enduring influence on the Catholic Church.] I cannot come to the Midlands without remembering that great man of God, that pilgrim for truth, Cardinal John Henry Newman. His quest for God and for the fullness of truth — a sign of the Holy Spirit at work within him — brought him to a prayerfulness and a wisdom which still inspires us today. Indeed Cardinal Newman's many years of seeking a fuller understanding of the faith reflect his abiding confidence in the words of Christ: 'I shall ask the Father and he will give you another Advocate to be with you forever, that Spirit of truth whom the world can never receive since it neither sees nor knows him' (John 14: 16,17). And so I commend to you [Cardinal Newman's] example of persevering faith and longing for the truth. He can help you to draw nearer to God, in whose presence he lived, and to whose service he gave himself totally. His teaching has great importance today in our search for

Christian unity too, not only in this country but throughout the world. Imitate his humility and his obedience to God; pray for a wisdom like his, a wisdom that can come from God alone.

SPEKE AIRPORT, LIVERPOOL, 30 MAY

The Pope was greeted by a crowd of over 150,000 people when he arrived at Speke Airport in the middle of the afternoon. Before being driven slowly through the crowds the Pope delivered a short address, during which he said:

Our times present us with many challenges and difficulties. One problem in particular which I would like to mention is unemployment. I know that you are experiencing this very seriously in Liverpool, and it is one of the major problems facing society as a whole. In many countries, unemployment has risen sharply and caused hardship to individuals and families. It tends to sow seeds of bitterness, division and even violence. The young, unable to find a job, feel cheated of their dreams, while those who have lost their jobs feel rejected and useless. This tragedy affects every aspect of life, from the material and physical to the mental and spiritual. It therefore very much concerns the Church, which makes her own the hardships and sufferings, as well as the joys and hopes, of the men and women of our time. It is a matter of vital importance and it deserves the attention and prayers of all people of good will. . . .

I have been told that as I travel through Liverpool our motorcade will be passing along Hope Street. This name struck me immediately as an expression of the aspirations of the people who live here, an expression of their hope for the future, especially for the future of their children and their children's children. So many dangers and problems face our young people today. I have already mentioned unemployment. In addition there are such evils as alcoholism and drug addiction, pornography, misguided notions of sexuality, and increasing crime and violence.

All these ills of society could bring us to disillusionment and even despair, if we were not a people of hope, if we did not have a deep and abiding confidence in the power and mercy of God. And so our young people, indeed all of us, need the virtue of hope, a hope founded not on fantasy and dreams, not even on what is seen, but a hope which arises from our faith in the God who loves us and is our gentle and merciful Father.

VISIT TO THE ANGLICAN CATHEDRAL, LIVERPOOL, 30 MAY

Large crowds lined the Pope's six-mile route into the centre of Liverpool. His journey

In Manchester the Pope ordained twelve priests at an open-air Mass in Heaton Park, 31 May

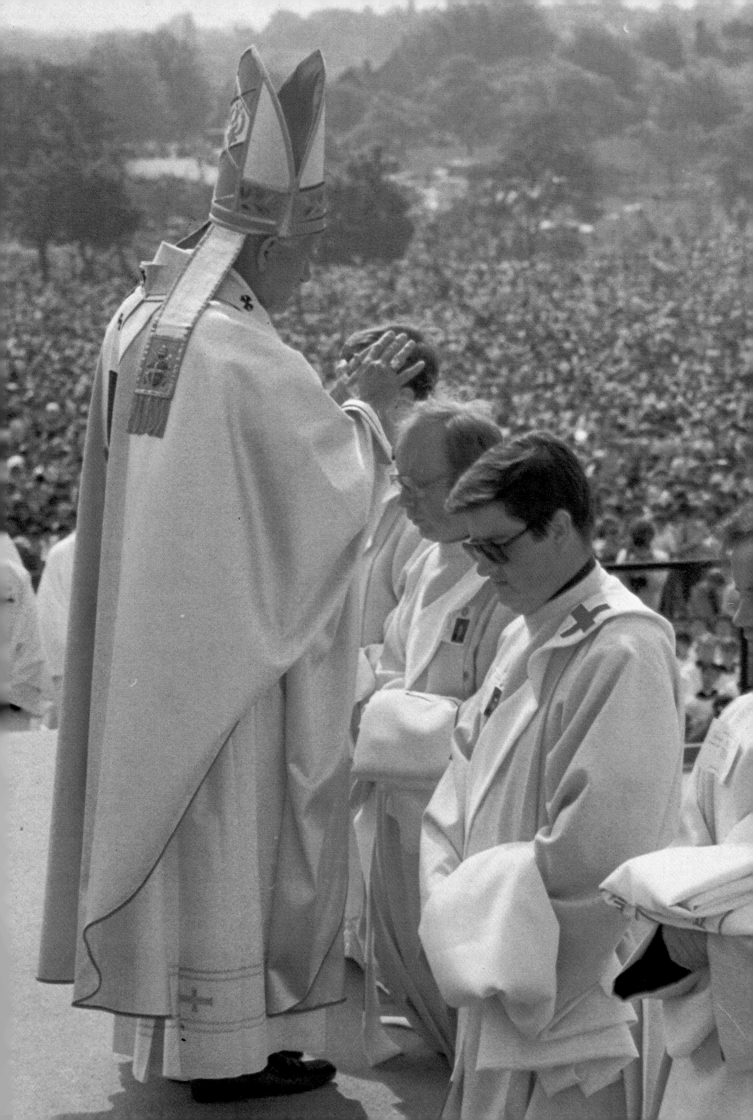

to the Metropolitan Cathedral of Christ the King took him through Toxteth, the scene of street rioting in the summer of 1981. On the way he stopped briefly to take part in a service at the Anglican Cathedral, where he was welcomed by the Rt Rev. David Shepherd, Bishop of Liverpool, who has worked closely with Archbishop Worlock over several years to bring Catholics and Protestants closer together in a city of deep-seated, extreme and often opposing views. The Pope greeted church leaders from Merseyside and exchanged a sign of peace with them before leading the congregation in the recitation of the Lord's Prayer.

MASS AT THE METROPOLITAN CATHEDRAL OF CHRIST THE KING, LIVERPOOL, 30 MAY

Reconciliation

The Pope travelled along Hope Street to the Metropolitan Cathedral where he was welcomed by the Most Rev. Derek Worlock, Archbishop of Liverpool. In the magnificent splendour of the modern cathedral, scene of the National Pastoral Congress in 1980, the Pope celebrated the Mass of Pentecost for two thousand Catholics drawn from throughout the northern Province.

As Pentecost Sunday draws to its close, we have come to this Church, the Cathedral Church of Christ the King, here in Liverpool, to celebrate the Holy Eucharist, the source and summit of Christian life and the Sacrament of unity and love. . . .

Although it is not possible this evening to celebrate the Sacrament of Penance, nevertheless I wish to emphasise the importance of penance and reconciliation in the life of the Church and in the lives of all her individual members. . . .

There is no sin which cannot be forgiven, if we approach the throne of mercy with humble and contrite hearts. No evil is more powerful than the infinite mercy of God. In becoming man, Jesus entered completely into our human experience, even to the point of suffering the final and most cruel effect of the power of sin — death on a Cross. He really became one like us in all things but sin. But evil with all its power did not win. By dying, Christ destroyed our death; by rising, he restored our life; by his wounds we are healed and our sins are forgiven. For this reason, when the Lord appeared to his disciples after the Resurrection, he showed them his hands and his side. He wanted them to see that the victory had been won; to see that he, the Risen Christ, had transformed the marks of sin and death into symbols of hope and life. . . .

On this day of Pentecost, as the Church proclaims the reconciling action of Christ Jesus, and the power of his Holy Spirit, I appeal to all the faithful of

84

> Britain — and to all the other members of the Church who may hear my voice or read my words: Dearly beloved, let us give greater emphasis to the Sacrament of Penance in our own lives. . . .
>
> As Christians today strive to be sources of reconciliation in the world, they feel the need, perhaps more urgently than ever before, to be fully reconciled among themselves. For the sin of disunity among Christians, which has been with us for centuries, weighs heavily upon the Church. . . .
>
> Restoration of unity among Christians is one of the main concerns of the Church in the last part of the twentieth century. And this task is for all of us. No one can claim exemption from this responsibility. Indeed everyone can make some contribution, however small it may seem, and all are called to that interior conversion which is the essential condition for ecumenism.

After the Mass the Pope was greeted in words and song by two thousand of the city's young people gathered in the Cathedral Piazza. He addressed them briefly, and then joined them in singing 'Bind us together, Lord'.

The Pope spent the night at Archbishop's House, Liverpool.

MASS AT HEATON PARK, MANCHESTER, 31 MAY
Ordination to the Priesthood

Before a Mass at Heaton Park, attended by about 200,000 people, the Pope met the Chief Rabbi of the United Kingdom and Commonwealth, Sir Immanuel Jakobovits, and other leaders of the Jewish Community at the nearby Convent of the Poor Sisters of Nazareth. During the Mass the Pope ordained twelve men to the priesthood.

> To be a new creation is the vocation of all the baptised. . . . Every believer is called to discipleship. By steadfastness in prayer, by compassion for those in need, by concern for justice in human affairs, Christians exercise the priesthood of the faithful, a living fellowship in Christ offering praise and glory to God our Father.
>
> But if we can apply the attributes of this new order of creation to the priesthood of the faithful, how much more compelling is their application to the ministerial or hierarchical priesthood, which is directed towards the sanctification of God's people. . . .
>
> You must be men of God, his close friends. You must develop daily patterns of prayer, and penance must be a regular part of your life. Prayer and penance will help you to appreciate more deeply that the strength of your ministry is found in the Lord and not in human resources. . . .
>
> You must try to deepen every day your friendship with Christ. You must also

Overleaf: **The Pope acknowledges the crowds at Knavesmire Racecourse, York, 31 May**

learn to share the hopes and the joys, the sorrows and the frustrations of the people entrusted to your care. Bring to them Christ's saving message of reconciliation. Visit your parishioners in their homes. This has been a strength of the Church in England. It is a pastoral practice that should not be neglected. Teach your people boldly about the faithful love of God. You must show that you believe in that faithful love by the fidelity with which you live your own life. You must proclaim the Gospel with your life. When you celebrate the sacraments at the decisive moments of their lives, help them to trust in Christ's promised mercy and compassion. When you offer the redeeming Sacrifice of the Eucharist, help them to understand the need for transforming this great love into works of charity. . . .

The Church, too, must be a family, bishops, priests, deacons, religious and laity, supporting each other and sharing with each other the individual gifts given by God. Every priest relies on the faith and talents of his parish community. If he is wise he will not only know the joy of dispensing God's grace, but also of receiving it abundantly through his parishioners as well. The partnership between priests and people is built upon prayer, collaboration and mutual respect and love. That has always been the tradition of these islands. May it never be lost.

KNAVESMIRE RACECOURSE, YORK, 31 MAY
Renewal of Marriage Vows

This morning in Manchester, young men were ordained to the sacred priesthood of Christ. They were answering the call of God's love. For many people, as for Margaret Clitheroe [martyred for her faith in York during 1586] , that call from God comes in and through marriage and family life. This is our theme. In our liturgical setting, which calls to mind the supremacy of God's saving grace, you married people will be invited to renew the promises you first made on your wedding day.

In a marriage a man and a woman pledge themselves to one another in an unbreakable alliance of total mutual self-giving. A total union of love. Love that is not a passing emotion or temporary infatuation, but a responsible and free decision to bind oneself completely, 'in good times and in bad', to one's partner. It is the gift of oneself to the other. It is a love to be proclaimed before the eyes of the whole world. It is unconditional.

To be capable of such love calls for careful preparation from early childhood to wedding day. It requires the constant support of Church and society throughout its development. The love of husband and wife in God's plan leads beyond itself and new life is generated, a family is born. The family is a community of love and life, a home in which children are guided to maturity.

Marriage is a holy sacrament. Those baptised in the name of the Lord Jesus are married in his name also. Their love is a sharing in the love of God. He is its source. The marriages of Christian couples, today renewed and blessed, are images on earth of the wonder of God, the loving, life-giving communion of Three Persons in one God, and of God's covenant in Christ, with the Church.

Christian marriage is a sacrament of salvation. It is the pathway to holiness for all members of a family. With all my heart, therefore, I urge that your homes be centres of prayer; homes where families are at ease in the presence of God; homes to which others are invited to share hospitality, prayer and the praise of God: 'With gratitude in your hearts sing psalms and hymns and inspired songs to God; and never say or do anything except in the name of the Lord Jesus Christ, giving thanks to God the Father through him' (Colossians 3:16,17).

In your country, there are many marriages between Catholics and other baptised Christians. Sometimes these couples experience special difficulties. To these families I say: You live in your marriage the hopes and difficulties of the path to Christian unity. Express that hope in prayer together, in the unity of love. Together invite the Holy Spirit of love into your hearts and into your homes. He will help you to grow in trust and understanding.

Brothers and sisters, 'May the peace of Christ reign in your hearts . . . let the message of Christ, in all its richness, find a home with you' (Colossians 3:15,16).

Recently I wrote an Apostolic Exhortation to the whole Catholic Church regarding the role of the Christian Family in the modern world. In that Exhortation I underlined the positive aspects of family life today, which include: a more lively awareness of personal freedom and greater attention to the quality of interpersonal relationships in marriage, greater attention to promoting the dignity of women, to responsible procreation, to the education of children. But at the same time I could not fail to draw attention to the negative phenomena: a corruption of the idea and experience of freedom, with consequent self-centredness in human relations; serious misconceptions regarding the relationship between parents and children; the growing number of divorces; the scourge of abortion; the spread of a contraceptive and anti-life mentality. Besides these destructive forces, there are social and economic conditions which affect millions of human beings, undermining the strength and stability of marriage and family life. In addition there is the cultural onslaught against the family by those who attack married life as 'irrelevant' and 'outdated'. All of this is a serious

89

Pope John Paul responding to the Scottish youth at Murrayfield, Edinburgh

challenge to society and to the Church. As I wrote then: 'History is not simply a fixed progression towards what is better, but rather an event of freedom, and even a struggle between freedoms that are in mutual conflict.'

Married couples, I speak to you of the hopes and ideals that sustain the Christian vision of marriage and family life. You will find the strength to be faithful to your marriage vows in your love for God and your love for each other and for your children. Let this love be the rock that stands firm in the face of every storm and temptation. What better blessing could the Pope wish for your families than what Saint Paul wished for the Christians of Colossae: 'Be clothed in sincere compassion, in kindness and humility, gentleness and patience. Bear with one another; forgive each other as soon as a quarrel begins. The Lord has forgiven you; now you must do the same. Over all these clothes . . . put on love' (Colossians 3:12-14).

Being a parent today brings worries and difficulties, as well as joys and satisfactions. Your children are your treasure. They love you very much, even if they sometimes find it hard to express that love. They look for independence and are reluctant to conform. Sometimes they wish to reject past traditions and even reject their faith.

In the family, bridges are meant to be built, not broken; and new expressions of wisdom and truth can be fashioned from the meeting of experience and enquiry. Yours is a true and proper ministry in the Church. Open the doors of your home and of your heart to all the generations of your family.

We cannot overlook the fact that some marriages fail. But still it is our duty to proclaim the true plan of God for all married love and to insist on fidelity to that plan, as we go towards the fullness of life in the Kingdom of heaven. Let us not forget that God's love for his people, Christ's love for the Church, is everlasting and can never be broken. And the covenant between a man and a woman joined in Christian marriage is as indissoluble and irrevocable as this love. This truth is a great consolation for the world, and because some marriages fail, there is an ever greater need for the Church and all her members to proclaim it faithfully.

Christ himself, the living source of grace and mercy, is close to all those whose marriage has known trial, pain, or anguish. Throughout the ages countless married people have drawn from the Paschal Mystery of Christ's Cross and Resurrection the strength to bear Christian witness — at times very difficult — to the indissolubility of Christian marriage. And all the efforts of the Christian people to bear faithful witness to God's law, despite human weakness, have not been in vain. These efforts are the human response made, through grace, to a God who has first loved us and who has given himself for us.

94

Pope John Paul greets one of the young people of Scotland at Murrayfield

As I explained in my Apostolic Exhortation *Familiaris Consortio*, the Church is vitally concerned for the pastoral care of the family in all difficult cases. We must reach out with love — the love of Christ — to those who know the pain of failure in marriage; to those who know the loneliness of bringing up a family on their own; to those whose family life is dominated by tragedy or by illness of mind or body. I praise all those who help people wounded by the breakdown of their marriage, by showing them Christ's compassion and counselling them according to Christ's truth.

To the public authorities, and to all men and women of good will, I say: treasure your families. Protect their rights. Support the family by your laws and administration. Allow the voice of the family to be heard in the making of your policies. The future of your society, the future of humanity, passes by way of the family.

My brothers and sisters in Christ, who are now about to renew the promises of your wedding day: may your words express once more the truth that is in your heart and may they generate faithful love within your families. Make sure that your families are real communities of love. Allow that love to reach out to other people, near and far. Reach out especially to the lonely and burdened people of your neighbourhood, to the poor and to all those on the margin of society. In this way you will build up your society in peace, for peace requires trust, and trust is the child of love, and love comes to birth in the cradle of the family.

Today and always, may God bless all of you, and all the families of Britain. Amen.

Thousands of couples in a crowd of nearly 250,000 people renewed their marriage vows during the Pope's last event in England. He left the racecourse by helicopter for RAF Leeming, and from there continued his pilgrimage to Scotland.

SCOTLAND

SCOTTISH NATIONAL YOUTH PILGRIMAGE, MURRAYFIELD, EDINBURGH, 31 MAY

On his arrival at RAF Turnhouse, Edinburgh, the Pope kissed the ground of Scotland. After being welcomed by Cardinal Gordon Gray, Archbishop of St Andrews and Edinburgh, and members of the Scottish hierarchy the Pope was driven to Murrayfield Stadium, where over 40,000 young people from all over Scotland gave him the most exuberant, enthusiastic and emotional welcome of his visit to Britain. Cardinal Gray introduced them with the words, 'Dear Holy Father, I bring you the young Catholics

The historic meeting between Pope John Paul II and the Moderator of the General Assembly of the Church of Scotland in the forecourt of the Assembly Hall, Edinburgh, 31 May

of Scotland'. They chanted 'John Paul, John Paul', applauded nearly every sentence of his address, and sang 'You'll Never Walk Alone'.

Dear young people of Scotland!

Thank you for your welcome, for the words and for the song. I am happy that my first contact is with you, the pride of your beloved country and the promise of its bright future!

You are at the great crossroads of your lives and you must decide how your future can be lived happily, accepting the responsibilities which you hope will be placed squarely on your shoulders. You ask me for encouragement and guidance, and most willingly I offer some words of advice to all of you, in the name of Jesus Christ.

In the first place I say this: you must never think that you are alone in deciding your future!

And secondly: when deciding your future, you must not decide for yourself alone! . . .

Left alone to face the difficult challenges of life today, you feel conscious of your own inadequacy and afraid of what the future may hold for you. But what I say to you is this: place your lives in the hands of Jesus. He will accept you, and bless you, and he will make such use of your lives as will be beyond your greatest expectations! . . .

It is not of primary importance what walk of life naturally attracts you — industry or commerce, science or engineering, medicine or nursing, the priestly or religious life, or the law, or teaching, or some other form of public service — the principle remains always the same: hand the direction of your life over to Jesus and allow him to transform you and obtain the best result, the one he wishes from you.

Only Christianity has given a religious meaning to work and recognises the spiritual value of technological progress. There is no vocation more religious than work! . . .

The clearest description of the work of the Holy Spirit has been given by Saint Paul, who said that the Spirit produces 'love, joy, peace, patience, kindness, goodness, trustfulness, gentleness and self-control' (Galatians 5:22). Qualities such as these are ideal in every walk of life and in all circumstances: at home, with your parents and brothers and sisters; at school, with your teachers and friends; in the factory or at the university; with all the people you meet. . . .

An exclusively personal and private attitude to salvation is not Christian and is born of a fundamentally mistaken mentality.

Consequently, your lives cannot be lived in isolation, and even in deciding

Pope John Paul and Cardinal Gordon Gray kneel in silent prayer

your future you must always keep in mind your responsibility as Christians towards others. There is no place in your lives for apathy or indifference to the world around you. There is no place in the Church for selfishness. You must show a conscientious concern that the standards of society fit the plan of God. Christ counts on you, so that the effects of his Holy Spirit may radiate from you to others and in that way permeate every aspect of the public and the private sector of national life. 'To each is given the manifestation of the Spirit for the common good' (1 Corinthians 12:7).

Do not let the sight of the world in turmoil shake your confidence in Jesus. Not even the threat of nuclear war. Remember his words: 'Be brave: I have conquered the world' (John 16:33). Let no temptation discourage you. Let no failure hold you down. There is nothing that you cannot master with the help of the One who gives you strength.

MEETING WITH THE MODERATOR OF THE GENERAL ASSEMBLY OF THE CHURCH OF SCOTLAND, 31 MAY

The historic meeting between the Moderator of the General Assembly of the Church of Scotland, the Rt Rev. Professor John McIntyre, and the Pope took place in the courtyard of the Church of Scotland Assembly Hall in the shadow of the statue of John Knox, leader of the Scottish Reformation.

In a short address of welcome the Moderator said: 'From this spirit of reconciliation which informs our meeting today, we, for our part, look forward to further dialogue with your church not only on topics of disagreement but also on joint themes on which we agree.'

This brief meeting took place en route from Murrayfield to St Mary's Cathedral, where the Pope addressed Scottish clergy and religious before going to St Bennet's, Cardinal Gray's residence, where he stayed for two nights. Large crowds on either side of Princes Street, closed for the occasion, gave the Pope a memorable welcome to the capital of Scotland.

MEETING WITH SCOTTISH CHURCH LEADERS, EDINBURGH, 1 JUNE

The Pope had a private meeting with the Moderator of the General Assembly of the Church of Scotland at Cardinal Gray's house. Later they were joined by other Scottish church leaders, and during his formal address to them the Pope said:

... soon after my arrival in Scotland, I had the happiness of being greeted by the Moderator of the General Assembly of the Church of Scotland, the Right Reverend Professor John McIntyre. In this regard, I cannot fail to recall that first historic meeting in 1961 between the then Moderator, Dr Archibald Craig, and my own predecessor John XXIII; or the courtesy of Dr Peter Brodie during his Moderatorial year in attending, in 1978, both my own installation and that of John Paul I. I am aware too of the significance of last night's happy venue, the precincts of the Assembly Hall itself, the seat of the Church of Scotland's Supreme Court, and also the *locus* of that momentous meeting in 1910 of the World Missionary Conference which is generally regarded as marking the beginning of the modern Ecumenical Movement. . . .

In particular I have been pleased to learn of the fruitful dialogue in which the Catholic Church in this country has been engaged with the Church of Scotland, the Episcopal Church in Scotland and other Churches, and also of its collaboration with the Scottish Churches' Council in many aspects of its work. I would like to make special mention of the Joint Commissions on Doctrine and on Marriage with the Church of Scotland and the Joint Study Group with the Scottish Episcopal Church, members of which groups are present here this morning. May I express my appreciation for your patient and painstaking work in the name of Christ. Here too we have an instance of that common witness which is both an expression of the degree of unity, limited but real, which we already enjoy through God's grace, and of our sincere desire to follow the ways by which God is leading us to that full unity which he alone can give. In following this road we have still to overcome many obstacles occasioned by the sad history of past enmities, we have to resolve important doctrinal issues; yet already mutual love, our will for unity, can be a sign of hope to a divided world — not least in these days in which peace is so sorely imperilled.

VISIT TO ST JOSEPH'S HOSPITAL FOR THE SEVERELY HANDICAPPED, ROSEWELL, NEAR EDINBURGH, 1 JUNE

After touring the wards and meeting many of the residents and staff of the hospital, Pope John Paul gave these words of encouragement:

Those who do not enjoy the fullness of what is called a normal way of life, through either mental or serious physical handicap, are often compensated in part by qualities which people often take for granted or even distort, under the influence of a materialistic society: such things as a radiant love — transparent, innocent and yearning — and the attraction of loving and selfless care. In this regard, we often find in the Gospels the refreshing example of Jesus himself, and the loving bond of affection between him and the sick or disabled: how many were his exertions for them, the great words of faith addressed to them, and his wonderful interventions on their behalf, 'for power came forth from him' (Luke 6:19; cf. Mark 1:32-34). There were times when he went out of his way to

101

identify himself with the sick and the suffering, he who was to suffer such a Passion and death himself: 'I was sick and you visited me . . . As you did it to one of the least of these my brethren, you did it to me' (Matthew 25:36,40).

These latter words of Jesus are also a source of great consolation to all those who care for the sick and disabled: nurses and medical staff, sisters and chaplains, parents, voluntary helpers and friends.

VISIT TO ST ANDREW'S COLLEGE, BEARSDEN, GLASGOW, 1 JUNE

Students and teachers from educational institutions throughout the country gathered at Scotland's only Roman Catholic teacher training college to hear the Pope give an address on education.

It would seem to be the case that in modern times the success of a particular educational programme or system has been measured, to a large extent, by the recognised qualification it provides with a view to some career-prospect. . . .

But nowadays, as we have been made only too aware, the possession of a certificate does not bring automatic employment. Indeed, this harsh reality has brought about not only deep frustration among young people, many of whom have worked so hard, but also a sense of malaise in the educational system itself. Hence the question: what has gone wrong? What has specialisation achieved in our day — in real terms, in terms of life? Wherein lies the remedy?

Perhaps we could reflect on the philosophy behind education: education as the completing of the person. To be educated is to be more fitted for life; to have a greater capacity for appreciating what life is, what it has to offer, and what the person has to offer in return to the wider society of man. Thus, if we would apply our modern educational skills and resources to this philosophy, we might succeed in offering something of lasting value to our pupils and students, an antidote to often immediate prospects of frustration and boredom, not to mention the uncertainty of the long-term future.

I am given to understand that educationists and educational authorities in Scotland have already come to terms with this problem and are giving due emphasis to education as development of the whole person; not only intellectual ability, but also emotional, physical and social development. . . .

In reflecting on the value of Catholic schools and the importance of Catholic teachers and educators, it is necessary to stress the central point of Catholic education itself. Catholic education is above all a question of communicating Christ, of helping to form Christ in the lives of others. Those who have been baptised must be trained to live the newness of Christian life in justice and in the

Pope John Paul arrives at Bellahouston Park, Glasgow, 1 June
Overleaf: **The crowds and trees at Bellahouston Park provide a colourful backdrop for a procession of priests**

holiness of truth. The cause of Catholic education is the cause of Jesus Christ and of his Gospel at the service of man.

NATIONAL MASS FOR SCOTLAND, BELLAHOUSTON PARK, GLASGOW, 1 JUNE

On a glorious summer day the Most Rev. Thomas Winning, Archbishop of Glasgow, welcomed Pope John Paul to Bellahouston Park where nearly 300,000 people from all over Scotland gave the Holy Father a tumultuous welcome. At the end of an unforgettable Mass they sang 'Will Ye No Come Back Again?'. At one point during the Pope's address the crowd, the largest ever assembled in Scotland, applauded him for nearly eight minutes.

We are gathered here on this Scottish hillside to celebrate Mass. Are we not like those first disciples and followers who sat at the feet of Jesus on the hillside near Capernaum? What did Jesus teach them? What does our divine Master wish to teach us, each and every one of us, today? With words simple and clear, Jesus outlined the requirements for admission to his heavenly Kingdom. He offered reflections on every aspect of daily life. Jesus proposed a new concept of living. In the short introductory phrases to his Sermon on the Mount, Jesus sounded the keynote of the New Era he had come to proclaim.

The new spirit is to be gentle, generous, simple, and above all sincere. To avoid being arrogant, censorious, or self-seeking. The disciples of the new Kingdom must seek happiness even amidst poverty, deprivation, tears and oppression. To aim for the Kingdom requires a radical change in outlook, in mentality, in behaviour, in relations with others. Just as the Law was revealed to Moses on Mount Sinai, so, in this Sermon on the Mount, Jesus, the new Lawgiver, offers to all mankind a new way of life, a charter of Christian life. . . .

Dear beloved Catholics of Scotland, the prayers of your forefathers did not go unanswered! Their firm hope in divine providence was not disillusioned! . . . With grateful hearts turn to God and thank him that tranquil days have been restored to the Catholic community in Scotland.

What was a dream a century ago has become the reality of today. A complete transformation of Catholic life has come about in Scotland, with the Catholics of Scotland assuming their legitimate role in every sector of public life and some of them invested with the most important and prestigious offices of this land. . . .

The spirit of this world would have us capitulate on the most fundamental principles of our Christian life. Today as never before, the basic doctrines of the Faith are questioned and the value of Christian morality challenged and ridiculed. Things abhorred a generation ago are now inscribed in the statute books of society! . . .

The Pope and the Most Rev. Thomas Winning, Archbishop of Glasgow, in the special papal vehicle at Bellahouston Park, Glasgow

To provide the answers to such questions is a daunting task. It would be an impossible challenge for the majority of the faithful to attempt unaided. But you are not alone. The Spirit of God is operative in the Church. Never before as in recent years has the teaching of the Catholic Church been so extensively reformulated, precisely with the issues that trouble the modern conscience in mind. It is sufficient to list the topics on which the Popes, the Ecumenical Council, the Synod of Bishops, and the various national Episcopal Conferences, including that of the Scottish Bishops, have given authoritative and clear statements of Catholic belief and practice for the guidance of the faithful in these perplexing times. In the name of all the shepherds of Christ's flock, to whom the office of pastors and teachers has been divinely entrusted (Ephesians 4:11), I assure you that we are acutely aware of the problems you have to face in life, and of the anxiety which so often fills your hearts. . . .

Beloved sons and daughters! I have been kept fully informed of the careful preparations, spread over many months, which have preceded my pastoral visit to Scotland. With admiration and satisfaction I have followed the intense programme proposed by the Bishops for a spiritual renewal of the Catholic community, to ensure that the effects of my visit produce fruits that will endure. From the depths of my heart I thank each and every one of you for the prayers that have accompanied this preparation, for every effort that has been made to guarantee its success. 'This is the day made memorable by the Lord: what immense joy for us' (Psalms 118:24). I commend you all, Bishops, clergy, religious and laity to the maternal intercession of Mary, the Immaculate Mother of God and Mother of the Church.

Before concluding, I wish to address for a few moments that larger community of believers in Christ, who share with my Catholic brothers and sisters the privilege of being Scots, sons and daughters alike of this ancient nation. I know of the veneration in which you hold the Sacred Scriptures, accepting them for what they are, the word of God, and not of man. I have reserved until now and should like to read to you the remaining words from that passage of Saint Paul's letter to the Ephesians: 'There is one body, one Spirit, just as you were all called into one and the same hope when you were called. There is one Lord, one Faith, one baptism, and one God who is Father of all, over all, through all and within all' (Ephesians 4:5,6). This passage clearly reveals the will of God for mankind, a plan which human wills may oppose but cannot thwart. It is God's plan for all of us, 'for there is no eternal city for us in this life but we look for one in the life to come' (Hebrews 13:15). We are only pilgrims on this earth, making our way towards that heavenly Kingdom promised to us as God's children. Beloved brethren in Christ, for the future, can we not make that pilgrimage together hand-in-hand, 'bearing with one another charitably, in complete selflessness, gentleness and patience', doing all we can 'to preserve the unity of the Spirit by the peace that binds us together' (Ephesians 4:2,3)? This would surely bring down upon us the blessing of God our Father on our pilgrim way.

WALES

MASS AT PONTCANNA FIELDS, CARDIFF, 2 JUNE
First Communion

On his arrival at Rhoose Airport, Cardiff, the Pope kissed the ground of Wales as a male voice choir sang 'We'll Keep a Welcome in the Hillside'. The total Catholic population of Wales is a mere 150,000, but a crowd estimated at 100,000 heard the Most Rev. John Murphy, Archbishop of Cardiff, welcome Pope John Paul to Pontcanna Fields.

In his homily, part of which he delivered in Welsh, the Pope said:

Today the Bishop of Rome greets the people of Wales for the first time in their own beautiful land. It is a great joy for me to be with you here in Cardiff. . . .

In Wales, the Eucharist has held a place of prominence in the Church from the earliest times. This is shown by the Christian symbols of the Eucharist which have been discovered in the archaeological excavations at the Roman fort of Caerleon. Happily this great heritage has continued from the early beginnings down to the present time. This fact should not surprise us, since the Eucharist holds such a central place in Christian life and since the mystery of the Eucharist is so closely linked to the mystery of the Church. For every generation in the Church, the food which nourishes the people of God is the Eucharist, the body and blood of Our Lord Jesus Christ. . . .

And now I would like to speak to these little ones who are about to receive Holy Communion for the first time. Dear children: Jesus is coming to you in a new way today, in a special way. He wants to live in you. He wants to speak to you in your heart. He wants to be with you all through your day.

Jesus comes to you in the Eucharist so that you will live for ever. Holy Communion is not ordinary food. It is the bread of eternal life. It is something more precious than gold or silver. It is worth more than anything you can imagine. For this sacred bread is the body and blood of Jesus. And Jesus promises that if you eat his flesh and drink his blood, you will have life in you and you will live for ever.

You come to the altar today with faith and prayer. Promise me that you will try

Overleaf: **The Papal Altar at Bellahouston Park**

to stay close to Jesus always, and never turn your back on him. As you grow older, go on learning about Jesus by listening to his word and by talking to him in prayer. If you stay close to him, you will always be happy. . . .

My brothers and sisters in Christ, every time we gather for the Eucharist, we take part in the great mystery of faith. We receive the bread of life and the cup of eternal salvation. This is the cause of our joy and the source of our hope. May this great mystery be for you and the whole Church in Wales the centre of your life and the way to eternal salvation in Christ Jesus our Lord. Amen.

At Cardiff Castle the Pope was given the Freedom of the City. When he met Welsh church leaders later, Pope John Paul in a common plea for unity said that he had 'been happy to learn of the degree of co-operation between Roman Catholics and members of other churches and communities in Wales, and of the part played by Catholic consultors and observers in the work of the Council of Churches in Wales.'

NATIONAL YOUTH EVENT, NINIAN PARK, CARDIFF, 2 JUNE

Smiling and relaxed, Pope John Paul listened as young people with scarves in the papal colours swayed from side to side while they sang 'He's Got the Whole World in His Hands'. During this, the last of his addresses, the Pope told 35,000 young people from the twenty-one dioceses of England and Wales:

As my visit to Britain draws to an end, I am happy that this last meeting is with you — the youth of England and Wales, you who are the hope of tomorrow.

Before I go away, there is something really important that I wish to emphasise. There is something very closely linked to the sacraments that I have celebrated, something that is very much a part of the Gospel message, something that is essential to your Christian lives. It is prayer. Prayer is so important that Jesus himself tells us 'Pray constantly' (Luke 21:36). . . .

My dear young people, it is through prayer that Jesus leads us to his Father. It is in prayer that the Holy Spirit transforms our lives. It is in prayer that we come to know God: to detect his presence in our souls, to hear his voice speaking through our consciences, and to treasure his gift to us of personal responsibility for our lives and for our world.

It is through prayer that we can clearly focus our attention on the person of Jesus Christ and see the total relevance of his teaching for our lives. Jesus becomes the model for our actions, for our lives. We begin to see things his way.

Prayer transforms our individual lives and the life of the world. Young men and women, when you meet Christ in prayer, when you get to know his Gospel and reflect on it in relation to your hopes and your plans for the future, then

113

The offertory procession during Mass at Bellahouston Park, Glasgow

everything is new. Everything is different when you begin to examine in prayer the circumstances of every day, according to the set of values that Jesus taught. . . .

In prayer, united with Jesus — your brother, your friend, your Saviour, your God — you begin to breathe a new atmosphere. You form new goals and new ideals. Yes, in Christ you begin to understand yourselves more fully. . . .

In union with Jesus, in prayer, you will discover more fully the needs of your brothers and sisters. You will appreciate more keenly the pain and suffering that burden the hearts of countless people. Through prayer, especially to Jesus at Communion, you will understand so many things about the world and its relationship to him, and you will be in a position to read accurately what are referred to as the 'signs of the times'. Above all you will have something to offer those who come to you in need. Through prayer you will possess Christ and be able to communicate him to others. And this is the greatest contribution you can make in your lives: to communicate Christ to the world. . . .

It is my hope today, as I return to Rome, that you will remember why I came among you. And as long as the memory of this visit lasts, may it be recorded that I, John Paul II, came to Britain to call you to Christ, to invite you to pray !

DEPARTURE FROM GREAT BRITAIN

By the time Pope John Paul arrived at Cardiff Airport at the end of his six-day pastoral visit he had spoken more than thirty thousand words in public.

During his farewell before boarding the aircraft for Rome, the Pope concluded his visit with the following words:

My pastoral visit to the countries of Britain has now come to an end. I came here as a herald of peace, to proclaim a Gospel of peace and a message of reconciliation and love. I came also as a servant — the servant of Jesus Christ, my Saviour; and the servant, too, of the Christian people. As I have travelled round England, Scotland, and finally Wales, in fulfilment of my pastoral duty to confirm my brethren, I have sought to remind Catholics of the whole saving activity of Christ, the Redeemer, our Risen Lord. In each of the countries I have also been able to meet and to pray with our brethren from other Christian communities. For these wonderful opportunities and for the friendship and brotherly welcome I have received everywhere, I give praise to God and I thank you all. . . .

To all the people of England, Scotland and Wales, I say: May God bless you all. May he make you instruments of his peace, and may the peace of Christ reign in your hearts and in your homes. Thank you very much.

114

Ninian Park, Cardiff, 2 June: a thunderstorm engulfs Cardinal Hume (right, top) and the young of England and Wales as they await the Pope's arrival

REACTIONS

'Nothing will ever be the same again'

Nearly two million people flocked in person to see Pope John Paul II during his historic pastoral visit to Great Britain from Friday 28 May to Wednesday 2 June 1982. Though firm and strict in his pronouncements on matters of doctrine and morality, the Holy Father preached a gospel of love, compassion and peace wherever he went. He made history at Canterbury on 29 May when, as the first Pope ever to set foot on British soil, he took part in a Celebration of Faith in Canterbury Cathedral at the invitation of Dr Robert Runcie, the Archbishop of Canterbury. A few days later, at Bellahouston Park in Glasgow, the Pope said: 'We are only pilgrims on this earth. Can we not make this pilgrimage together hand-in-hand?'

Only time will give the answer to this vital question, but already one thing is certain. The Roman Catholic Church in Great Britain will never be the same again. As it stands at the dawn of a new era in its relationship with its beloved sister, the Church of England, the words of that great Englishman Cardinal Newman come to mind: 'I do not ask to see the distant scene — one step enough for me.'

The carefully considered views of leading churchmen which follow give an insight into the enormous impact made by Pope John Paul II.

The Most Rev. and Rt Hon. Robert Runcie,
Archbishop of Canterbury:

On the Sunday after the great Celebration of Faith in Canterbury Cathedral on 29 May it was said that 'the Pope and the Archbishop of Canterbury have blocked the way back'. Certainly things can never be the same again. The atmosphere has been changed and the Churches, as they professed together their common baptismal faith, were no longer seen in competition but as partners in the Gospel.

Yet the occasion was hardly complacent. While the Churches professed unity at the basic level of our baptismal faith, the cost of that faith in the twentieth century was pointed to in the modern martyrs, thus demonstrating the urgency of seeking the restoration of our broken unity. The theological, and now practical, discussions will continue, and I believe that the Pope's visit has helpfully shifted the ecumenical dialogue out of the exclusive domain of the experts to the parishes; to the priests and people as well as to the notables and prelates who were deeply moved by the Canterbury celebration. The Pope's sensitivity and attentiveness were clear for all to see. He has helped us to achieve a similar awareness of each other.

The Rev. Dr Philip Morgan, General Secretary of the
British Council of Churches:

Fulfilled hopes are always a cause for great joy. The papal visit was an occasion for such joy.

The sun breaks through the clouds as Pope John Paul begins the last major address of his visit

British church leaders had hoped to have a conversation with the Pope, and, sitting in a circle in the Deanery at Canterbury, they did so. The Pope listened intently to what was said and responded in a way which indicated that he had understood the issues being raised. In particular he agreed that the growing sense of spiritual communion must not be allowed to remain abstract. Ways had to be found to give it visible expression in the life of the churches. His appreciative references to co-operation between the Roman Catholic Church and the British Council of Churches indicated one possible way in which progress could be made.

In response to the conversation the Pope invited representatives of the BCC, together with representatives of the Episcopal Conferences of Great Britain, to continue the discussion in Rome. This linking of the hierarchies of England and Wales and Scotland with the BCC could be most important. The opportunity for continued conversation was warmly welcomed, though the form it will take has yet to be considered. In July the BCC Executive will respond to the invitation on behalf of the Council.

British church leaders had been realistic in their expectations of the Pope's visit: profound questions and historic differences were not likely to be settled in one brief conversation or even at one great service. It was felt however that doors could either be more firmly shut, or opened to future possibilities. There is general agreement that doors are now open to the future, and that is sufficient for the moment.

The Rt Rev. Alan Clark, Bishop of East Anglia:

No one has underestimated the impact of the papal visit on the ecumenical shape of the Church in England. Church leaders were invited to give their thoughts in advance, but the actual event, the words spoken, the personal stance of Pope John Paul, have eclipsed even the most sanguine aspirations of those who have at all times persevered in their dedication to Christian unity. Now, after the six-day visit, reflection is the order of the day, particularly in order to interpret what has happened to the Christian churches in Britain.

The Roman Catholic Church can have little doubt that the Bishop of Rome, whose charge it is to hold us all together in unity and truth, has committed us irrevocably to the path of reconciliation as the way to full communion. No longer can there be any waverings. Unity is possible, unity is our Christian duty, as is peace. The three transcendent values of unity, truth and love structured the Pope's frequent allusions to this overriding theme in his preaching, not only at Canterbury but elsewhere. There can be no going back without betrayal.

118

Top: **The Pope joins in the singing at Ninian Park together with Cardinal Hume, Cardinal Gray and other Church leaders**

Bottom: **A flurry of flags and an emotional farewell for the Pope as he departs for Cardiff airport**

Overleaf: **Young people from all over England and Wales parade with their church banners at Ninian Park**

But the going forward? It is to be 'together'. Hence the emphasis on the truth of the Christian faith and its doctrinal expression. When John Paul II said at Canterbury that he came with the love of Peter, with the love of Gregory and as a servant of unity, he expressed humbly but openly his own charge of confirming his brethren not only within the confines of the Roman Catholic Church but across the whole Christian communion. These were soul-searching words for all of us, yet positive and uncompromising. Yes, we are each and all justified by faith in Jesus Christ but this is a faith to be preached and practised. So any advance requires an integrity that is frequently undermined by conformity with secular values that insinuate themselves into today's Gospel preaching. A Roman Catholic, not exempt from such temptations, cannot however be free of anxiety regarding the thin doctrinal defences in the Christian churches and communities with whom he is charged to be the salt and light of the earth.

It is in this context that the programme outlined in the *Common Declaration* must be seen. Like ARCIC in its twelve years of labour, the new commission is no negotiating body but heralds the realities of faith on which depend for their integrity the practical consequences so eagerly desired by all.

The Spirit of God searches the hearts as well as the depths. It is in its environment that we are summoned to a daunting but glorious expedition led by the Lord of the Church and of the world. Discipleship is what binds us together now and will draw us closer — but not without the Cross.

The Most Rev. Thomas Winning, Archbishop of Glasgow:
When John Paul II came to Britain the spirit of God moved across the face of this island. It was a wind of change so palpably refreshing that the uncompromising but popular verdict, 'Things will never be the same again', seemed just about right.

The uncertainties surrounding the visit right up to the last minute only served to clarify for millions the real reasons for his coming: the people of Britain needed the presence of Pope John Paul to establish their priorities on a great number of issues.

He came to a country engaged in a bizarre conflict thousands of miles away which has stirred up embers of war fever we had considered long extinguished. Yet his first message was of peace and of an anathema to all wars.

John Paul exercises a genuine prophetic leadership because he has given himself totally to the Holy Spirit. His serenity, that restful attentiveness could only come from his being, as he himself confessed, a servant of God. His message then was not just for Catholics but for anyone who cared to heed him.

Children receive their First Communion during Mass at Pontcanna Fields, Cardiff, 2 June

In terms of example and witness the public had already deemed this visit an unqualified success, but clearly John Paul was looking for more than that. At Glasgow he warned against living in the past: 'But you do not live in the past. You belong to the present . . . You must give your response to Christ's call to follow him . . .'

In a sense the effects of his coming were already being felt up and down the country before he set foot in Britain, for the reaching out of the Church to those who had lapsed was bearing fruit in quite a considerable return to the Mass and Sacraments, to prayer and a deeper understanding of what being a Christian means.

Again, there has to be more than this. As far as the Catholic community is concerned an enduring response can only come from a personal openness to the work of the Holy Spirit and following from that a better appreciation of the Church's mission as it affects individuals of the whole community.

The Church cannot change Christ's message to conform with the fashions of the world. The media dubs John Paul a conservative, a reactionary, but what are its criteria for so doing? Unfortunately, they are the criteria of our present society which does not take kindly to prophetic challenges articulated in God's logic.

We cannot and should not, however, look for instant success. Conversion to God is conditioned by our receptivity. There are many of us who have still to open up in personal prayer to the promptings of the Spirit. After John Paul's visit this need for prayer assumes a new urgency. The people look to the teaching Church, to bishops and priests to give the lead. The latter might well take to themselves the words of our chief pastor: 'Dear brothers and sisters, preaching good news of Jesus is my life's work.'

The Most Rev. Derek Worlock, Archbishop of Liverpool:

During the long months of preparation for the papal visit more difficulties arose than we could ever have envisaged. Some were of far wider consequence than the visit itself: the assassination attempt and the South Atlantic conflict cast the whole enterprise into doubt. But there were other less specific problems of attitude — prejudice, fear, mistrust, misrepresentation, cynicism. As the projected date drew nearer I found myself saying repeatedly: 'When Pope John Paul comes, what he says, what he does and what he is, will be the total answer.'

Events proved that confident assertion fully justified. When he had completed his pilgrimage, no one asked any longer the meaning of a 'pastoral' visit because they had seen the chief pastor of the Church at work. No one questioned further

the reality of the so-called 'ecumenical aspect' of the visit because they had seen and experienced the Christian brotherhood exhibited by the Holy Father, who had given living expression to his teaching about the sacramental bond of unity linking all the baptised.

The teaching office of the successor of Peter could not have been spelled out more clearly than in the magnificent series of addresses delivered in the course of the visit. The catechetical content of his treatment of the sacraments of the Church will for years prove a rich treasury for the deepening of the knowledge and faith of priests and people alike. Always he spoke clearly and strongly but with a great sensitivity to local conditions and character. Uncompromising in truth, realistic and compassionate about current trends and challenges, he responded nobly to the demand to confirm our faith.

We saw Peter baptising new Christians, moving about among the sick, confirming, celebrating the Eucharist, ordaining, speaking of family life and reconciliation. We saw him responding to the outstretched hands of those who sought his very touch: his love and care for the handicapped and for little children: his fatherly counsel and sense of fun with young people. We drew encouragement from his patience, new sense of purpose from his total giving of himself, new values from his concern and respect for the humblest.

'What he says, what he does and most of all what he is. . .' My words kept coming back to me as in Cardiff I heard a commentary on the Pope's final foray among the crowd who had come to say goodbye. Struggling for words to describe the figure in white reaching down to the children, smiling, blessing, seemingly responding to each individual, the commentator said it all: 'He makes one think of Christ.'

Appendix

Succession of Roman Pontiffs

(The names of anti-popes are given in italic)

St Peter,
Prince of the Apostles
67 St Linus
76 St Anacletus or Cletus
88 St Clement
97 St Evaristus
105 St Alexander I
115 St Sixtus I
125 St Telesphorus
136 St Hyginus
140 St Pius I
155 St Anicetus
166 St Soter
175 St Eleutherius
189 St Victor I
199 St Zephyrinus
217 St Callistus I
217 St Hyppolytus
222 St Urban I
230 St Pontian
235 St Anterus
236 St Fabian
251 St Cornelius
251 Novatian
253 St Lucius I
254 St Stephen I
257 St Sixtus II
259 St Dionysius
269 St Felix I
275 St Eutychian
283 St Caius
296 St Marcellinus
308 St Marcellus I
309 St Eusebius
311 St Melchiades
314 St Silvester I
336 St Mark
337 St Julius I
352 Liberius
355 Felix II
366 St Damasus
366 Ursicinus
384 St Siricius
399 St Anastasius I
401 St Innocent I
417 St Zozimus
418 St Boniface I
418 Eulalius
422 St Celestine I
432 St Sixtus III
440 St Leo the Great
461 St Hilary
468 St Simplicius
483 St Felix III (II)
492 St Gelasius I
496 Anastasius II

498 St Symmachus
498 Lawrence
514 St Hormisdas
523 St John I
526 St Felix IV (III)
530 Boniface II
530 Dioscorus
533 John II
535 St Agapitus
536 St Silverius
537 Vigilius
556 Pelagius I
561 John III
575 Benedict I
579 Pelagius II
590 St Gregory the Great
604 Sabinian
607 Boniface III
608 St Boniface IV
615 St Deusdedit I
619 Boniface V
625 Honorius I
640 Severinus
640 John IV
642 Theodore I
649 St Martin I
654 St Eugene I
657 St Vitalian
672 Deusdedit II
676 Donus
678 St Agatho
682 St Leo II
684 St Benedict II
685 John V
686 Conon
687 Theodore
687 Paschal
687 St Sergius I
701 John VI
705 John VII
708 Sisinnius
708 Constantine
715 St Gregory II
731 St Gregory III
741 St Zachary
752 Stephen II (III)
757 St Paul I
767 Constantine
768 Philip
768 Stephen III (IV)
772 Adrian I
795 St Leo III
816 Stephen IV (V)
817 St Paschal I
824 Eugene II
827 Valentine

827 Gregory IV
844 John
844 Sergius II
847 St Leo IV
855 Benedict III
855 Anastasius
858 St Nicholas the Great
867 Adrian II
872 John VIII
882 Marinus I
884 St Adrian III
885 Stephen V (VI)
891 Formosus
896 Boniface VI
896 Stephen VI (VII)
897 Romanus
897 Theodore II
898 John IX
900 Benedict IV
903 Leo V
903 Christopher
904 Sergius III
911 Anastasius III
913 Landon
914 John X
928 Leo VI
928 Stephen VII (VIII)
931 John XI
936 Leo VII
939 Stephen VIII (IX)
942 Marinus II
946 Agapitus II
955 John XII
963 Leo VIII
964 Benedict V
965 John XIII
973 Benedict VI
974 Boniface VII
974 Benedict VII
983 John XIV
985 John XV
996 Gregory V
997 John XVI
999 Silvester II
1003 John XVII
1004 John XVIII
1009 Sergius IV
1012 Benedict VIII
1024 John XIX
1032 Benedict IX
1045 Sylvester III
1045 Benedict IX (2nd term)
1045 Gregory VI
1046 Clement II
1047 Benedict IX (3rd term)
1048 Damasus II

1049 St Leo IX
1055 Victor II
1057 Stephen X
1058 Benedict X
1059 Nicholas II
1061 Alexander II
1061 Honorius II
1073 St Gregory VII
1080 Clement III
1086 B Victor III
1088 B Urban II
1099 Pachal II
1100 Theoderic
1102 Albert
1105 Sylvester IV
1118 Gelasius II
1118 Gregory VIII
1119 Callistus II
1124 Honorius II
1124 Celestine II
1130 Innocent II
1130 Anacletus II
1138 Victor IV
1143 Celestine II
1144 Lucius II
1145 B Eugene III
1153 Anastasius IV
1154 Adrian IV
1159 Alexander III
1159 Victor IV
1164 Paschal III
1168 Callistus III
1179 Innocent III
1181 Lucius III
1185 Urban III
1187 Gregory VIII
1187 Clement III
1191 Celestine III
1198 Innocent III
1216 Honorius III
1227 Gregory IX
1241 Celestine IV
1243 Innocent IV
1254 Alexander IV
1261 Urban IV
1268 Clement IV
1271 B Gregory X
1276 B Innocent V
1276 Adrian V
1276 John XXI
1277 Nicholas III
1281 Martin IV
1285 Honorius IV
1288 Nicholas IV
1294 St Celestine V
1294 Boniface VIII

1303 B Benedict XI	1447 Nicholas V	1590 Urban VII	1758 Clement XIII
1305 Clement V	1455 Callistus III	1590 Gregory XIV	1769 Clement XIV
1316 John XXII	1458 Pius II	1591 Innocent IX	1775 Pius VI
1328 Nicholas V	1464 Paul II	1592 Clement VIII	1800 Pius VII
1334 Benedict XII	1471 Sixtus IV	1605 Leo XI	1823 Leo XII
1342 Clement VI	1484 Innocent VIII	1605 Paul V	1829 Pius VIII
1352 Innocent VI	1492 Alexander VI	1621 Gregory XV	1831 Gregory XVI
1362 B Urban V	1503 Pius III	1623 Urban VIII	1846 Pius IX
1371 Gregory XI	1503 Julius II	1644 Innocent X	1878 Leo XIII
1378 Urban VI	1513 Leo X	1655 Alexander VII	1903 St Pius X
1389 Boniface IX	1522 Adrian VI	1667 Clement IX	1914 Benedict XV
1404 Innocent VII	1523 Clement VII	1670 Clement X	1922 Pius XI
1406 Gregory XII	1534 Paul III	1676 B Innocent XI	1939 Pius XII
1378 Clement VII	1550 Julius III	1689 Alexander VIII	1958 John XXIII
1394 Benedict XIII	1555 Marcellus II	1691 Innocent XII	1963 Paul VI
1409 Alexander V	1555 Paul IV	1700 Clement XI	1978 John Paul I
1410 John XXIII	1559 Pius IV	1721 Innocent XIII	1978 **John Paul II**
1417 Martin V	1566 St Pius V	1724 Benedict XIII	
1431 Eugene IV	1572 Gregory XIII	1730 Clement XII	Based on the *Liber Pontificalis*,
1440 Felix V	1585 Sixtus V	1740 Benedict XIV	with corrections.

Succession of Archbishops of Canterbury

(In some instances dates assigned are only approximate)

597 **Augustine**	990 Sigeric Serio	1333 John Stratford	1678 William Sancroft
604 Laurentius	995 Aelfric	1349 Thomas Bradwardine	1691 John Tillotson
619 Mellitus	1005 Aelfheah	1349 Simon Islip	1695 Thomas Tenison
624 Justus	1013 Lyfing	1366 Simon Langham	1716 William Wake
627 Honorius	1020 Aethelnoth	1368 William Whittlesey	1737 John Potter
655 Deusdedit	1038 Eadsige	1375 Simon Sudbury	1747 Thomas Herring
668 Theodorus	1051 Robert of Jumièges	1381 William Courtenay	1757 Matthew Hutton
693 Beorhtweald	1052 Stigand	1396 Thomas Arundel	1758 Thomas Secker
731 Tatwine	1070 Lanfranc	1398 Roger Walden	1768 Frederick Cornwallis
735 Nothelm	1093 Anselm	1414 Henry Chichele	1783 John Moore
740 Cuthbeorht	1114 Ralph d'Escures	1443 John Stafford	1805 Charles Manners Sutton
761 Breguwine	1123 William de Corbeil	1452 John Kemp	1828 William Howley
765 Jaenbeorht	1139 Theobald	1454 Thomas Bourchier	1848 John Bird Sumner
793 Aethelheard	1162 Thomas Becket	1486 John Morton	1862 Charles Thomas Longley
805 Wulfred	1174 Richard (of Dover)	1501 Henry Dean	1868 Archibald Campbell Tait
832 Feologild	1185 Baldwin	1503 William Warham	1883 Edward White Benson
833 Ceolnoth	1193 Hubert Walter	1533 Thomas Cranmer	1896 Frederick Temple
870 Aethelred	1207 Stephen Langton	1556 Reginald Pole	1903 Randall Thomas Davidson
890 Plegmund	1229 Richard le Grant	1559 Matthew Parker	1928 Cosmo Gordon Lang
914 Aethelhelm	1234 Edmund Rich	1576 Edmund Grindall	1942 William Temple
923 Wulfhelm	1245 Boniface of Savoy	1583 John Whitgift	1945 Geoffrey Francis Fisher
942 Oda	1273 Robert Kilwarby	1604 Richard Bancroft	1961 Arthur Michael Ramsey
959 Aefsige	1279 John Pecham	1611 George Abbot	1974 Frederick Donald Coggan
959 Beorhthelm	1294 Robert Winchelsey	1633 William Laud	1980 **Robert Alexander**
960 Dunstan	1313 Walter Reynolds	1660 William Juxon	**Kennedy Runcie**
c.988 Athelgar	1328 Simon Mepeham	1663 Gilbert Sheldon	From *Crockford's Clerical Directory*.

PRINTED IN BELGIUM BY
proost
INTERNATIONAL BOOK PRODUCTION